Our Alaska

A pictorial history of the Great Land and its people

VOLUME II

TEXT WRITTEN BY MICHAEL CAREY
PHOTOS SUBMITTED BY READERS OF THE ANCHORAGE DAILY NEWS

PUBLISHED BY
THE ANCHORAGE DAILY NEWS
2003

PRINTED BY
QUEBECOR WORLD

(COVER PHOTO) A PILOT AND HIS WIFE TAKE A BREAK: Pilot Kenny Neese and his wife Mary are hoping to catch a few on the "boardwalk," Lake Otis, Anchorage 1938. The lake, now not much more than a pothole, is located west of 36th and what else - Lake Otis. Kenny began flying in Alaska in 1932, for McGee Airways. He was a bush pilot until 1941 when he and his family left Alaska. In 1967, a group of Anchorage aviation experts and enthusiasts named Kenny Neese one of the most important bush pilots in Alaska flying history. Kenny died in 1942, ferrying military aircraft. Mary Elizabeth Morford Neese lived until 1999. This day at the lake must have been one they both enjoyed and remembered. *(Submitted by Betty Neese Guyer)*

Preface

Welcome to Volume II of Our Alaska.

This is the second is a series of books that tell the story of Alaska through photographs. Volume I was published in 2001.

All the photos were supplied by Alaskans and Alaskan institutions - or Alaskans at heart who, for one reason or another, have relocated elsewhere.

A few photographs, including some of the earliest, were taken by professional photographers. A few more were taken by avid amateurs who seem to have felt that photography was essential to their lives. But most of the pictures were taken by everyday people as part of their everyday lives. With photographs, these Alaskans recorded their jobs, from early miners to modern construction workers, as well as birthdays, holidays, trips, family and neighborhood gatherings and annual events - the Anchorage Fur Rendezvous, the Fairbanks Winter Carnival, the Fourth Of July.

In other words, these photographs provide a portrait of Alaskans at work and play - and occasionally responding to crisis as in the photographs of the 1964 Good Friday earthquake.

For me, it was humbling that so many people would put the story of their lives and their families' lives in our hands. But clearly, people were willing to share their photographs because of the pride they feel in the photos and the stories accompanying them.

Perhaps it's true a good photograph is worth a thousand words, but show somebody a photograph, and they want to know the story behind it. The image may be interesting, even compelling, but the image needs context. Who are these people - and what happened to them? What is the occasion and why does it matter?

The captions and memorabilia in this volume serve the purpose of context - they illuminate the many stories people have to tell.

Every person is unique. Every photograph is too, even photos shot moments apart.

Our Alaska Volume II is a unique look at life on the Last Frontier. May you enjoy reading it just as much as we enjoyed putting it together for you.

Michael Carey
Editor

Corner Broadway and McKinley, Valdez, Alaska

All photos on these two pages submitted by Roberta Degenhardt

1125. Halibut Catch on Puget Sound.

STEAMER DAWSON, FIVE FINGER RAPIDS, ALASKA.

Pre-1920's

(LEFT) A GUEST GOES FISHING: Mrs. Silman, left, and her son have been fishing with Miss Bessie Wood. Bessie apparently was a visitor. The photo is before 1907 - that's what we know for sure. The back of the photo contains a note that identifies the women and says, "Our catch of Alaska salmon - trolled for." That must be downtown Seward in the background. *(Submitted by Iris and Hugh Darling)*

(ABOVE) IMPORTANT RESPONSIBILITIES, A TRAGIC END: John F. Pugh was the collector of customs for Alaska ports. It was an important job given the prominence of commerce by sea in the first quarter of the 20th century. Pugh, from Port Townsend, WA, died young, at age 44. He was a passenger on the doomed ship Princess Sophia, which sank October 24, 1918. Close to 350 people perished after the ship hit a reef near Juneau. The disaster affected families all over the territory of Alaska. A number of descendants of those who died still live here, including Pugh's grandson Karl Hahn. *(Submitted by Karl Hahn)*

(RIGHT) A MESSAGE TO THE FOLKS BACK HOME: Mary Kavanaugh, born Fox, was a nun who left the convent and married a gold miner. She was from New York City. Here she is writing to her brother in Manhattan. Mary was a great-great aunt to Roberta Degenhardt of Anchorage. Picture postcards have been popular with visitors for a long, long time. *(Submitted by Roberta Degenhardt)*

761 — AN ALASKAN DOG TEAM.

(LEFT) DOWNTOWN CITY COUNCIL: This team and wagon makes its way through the gold camp of Council City, 70 miles from Nome on the Seward Peninsula in 1908. Little Ruth Mary Markham (McDowell) born in Council in 1904 was one of the passengers. A Sister of Providence holds her. The Kane House (right) still stands. Ruth's mother worked at the Marks Hotel (in the background, middle). Her father, among other things, carried the mail by dog team. Ruth Mary visited Council City as recently as 1998. *(Submitted by Kathleen Hansen)*

(LEFT) PORTRAIT OF A STAMPEDER: Howard Porter was a true "stampeder." A Maine man, he left for Kotzebue Sound "when the gold excitement broke out in 1898" as a Maine newspaper put it in a story about him. Finding no gold, he became a merchant, opening a general mercantile store in Nome. He had a long career in Alaska, one that lasted into the 1940s when he had a store on 4th Avenue in Anchorage. At one point, Howard Porter mushed from Nome to Fairbanks and purchased horses that he drove to Valdez. The trip was arduous, long, and according to what he told the Maine newspaper, numerous travelers froze. Mr. Porter died in Maine, but he still has an Alaska connection. He is the great uncle of Ann Porter who lives in Anchorage. *(Submitted by Ann Porter)*

(ABOVE) AN OLD-FASHIONED BARN DANCE: It's 1924 and dancers at the community hall in Matanuska pause a moment for a group portrait. The fiddle player next to the man with the guitar is Fred Edlund, who homesteaded in the area in 1912. He is known to have had a large family. The photo is from the Frydenlund collection, donated to the Wasilla-Knik Historical Society by their daughter, Betty Frydenlund (Bryne), who visited Wasilla after a 70-year absence. *(Submitted by Wasilla-Knik Historical Society)*

(RIGHT) ONE HANDSOME FAMILY: It's portrait time for this distinguished family, perhaps in 1902. But for certain Benjamin A. Haldane who had a studio in Metlakatla took the photo. The back row is Rosa (Rosie) Baines, William Baines and Joel Baines. The front row is Mary Baines Hudson, the three Baines' sister, and her husband, John (Jonah) Hudson. Conrad Everett Hudson is between his parents. Also, Harold Cuthbert Hudson (on the right behind his father) and Laura Mary Hudson on father John's lap. Mary Baines Hudson, John (Jonah) Hudson, and Joel Baines all moved from Metlakatla B.C. (Canada) to Metlakatla, Alaska with Mary's parents the famed Anglican missionary William Duncan. Many of their descendants live in Alaska today. *(Submitted by David R. Baines)*

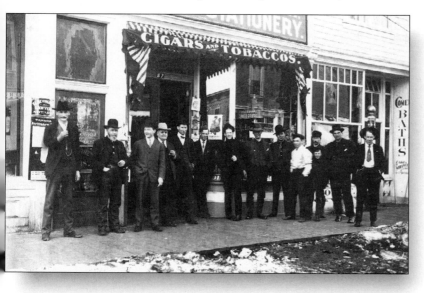

(ABOVE) THE SPORTS ALL GATHERED: The cigar store was a natural gathering place in frontier Alaska. These fellows are standing on the wooden sidewalk in front of a Fairbanks store about 1910. Note the hats. A gentleman had to have a hat. It is remarkable how quickly the tobacconists showed up in gold camps like Fairbanks. As soon as the first frame building went up, so did a sign "Cigars and tobacco" (or in this case "tobaccos."). *(Submitted by The Bruce Haldeman Collection)*

(BELOW) POPEYE AND HIS PAL: Robert Bertram Grassow, an officer of the revenue cutter Bear' in the teens and '20s, made many trips to Alaska. During a visit to King Island, he and others on the vessel showed local Natives the funny papers. Here's the result - Popeye and Wimpy, 8" tall in ivory. A skillful, imaginative King Islander apparently could not resist carving the international celebrities. The black used to highlight the detail is cigarette ash. *(Submitted by The Estate of Robert Bertram Grassow)*

SEWARD DIV GOV'T RAILROAD
-G- OCT 21 1918. J. RENO & FAMILY THE GIRDWOOD PIONEER.
A.E.C. 1060.

(ABOVE) GIRDWOOD OF YESTERYEAR: The Reno family is in the middle of Girdwood in 1918. Joe Reno is on the right, his wife on the left. Addie Reno is in the white dress. Sister Margie Reno is on the right. Jimmie Reno stands next to his dad. The names of other family members are uncertain. The Renos had a store in Girdwood - later had a grocery store at Fourth and C St. in Anchorage. Girdwood was named for a miner, James E. Girdwood, who came to the area in 1896. A post office was established in 1907. *(Submitted by Frank M. Reed)*

(RIGHT) A SCHOOL PHOTO OF LONG AGO: Emma Kininnook, age 13, stands for the camera at the Chimawa School near Salem, Ore. Chimawa was a boarding school for Native American youngsters. Emma was orphaned at a young age. At 14, she married Frank Williams, and they settled in Ketchikan. Frank fished; Emma was a mother, homemaker and occasionally worked in the canneries. The couple was married 67 years. Frank died at 87, Emma died at 99. *(Submitted by Harriett Fenerty)*

(ABOVE) NOT WHERE YOU WANT TO BE: The Princess May is on the rocks, Sentinel Island, north of Juneau, Aug. 10, 1910. This photo was converted into a postcard - for obvious reasons. Until just about World War I, Alaskans and visitors to Alaska could reach the Last Frontier only by sea. The Alaska Highway did not exist; air travel was in its infancy. Wrecks on the waves did occur but were rare. *(Submitted by Dorene Lorenz)*

(LEFT) A SONG TO SING: Montgomery (Monty) Snow was born in 1882 and came over the Chilkoot Pass with his parents and sister. The youngsters danced in Dawson's Grand Palace - their father was a performer in a musical stock company. But that wasn't Monty's only foray into the arts. He wrote "Alaska, My Alaska." The territorial song, as it has been called, joined the music of "Maryland, My Maryland" with Alaskanized lyrics. It was common all over the United States to re-write popular tunes by adding local lyrics (as in "It's A Long Way to Tipperary" became "It's A Long Way Across the Prairie"). To the modern ear this rewrite seems pretty stiff, as in the end of the first verse: "From Arctic Ocean's frozen shore/To Baranoff of Russian lore/Thy mighty rivers I adore/Alaska, my Alaska." *(Submitted by Paul Roseland)*

(ABOVE) A PICNIC WITH BERRIES: This group is apparently taking a little break from berry picking, sometime close to 1920. Carlotta Chisholm is on the left. Carlotta's husband, Jack, was a legendary salesman who made his home in Anchorage as early as 1915. With Carlotta are Mae Beattie, her sister, and Jessie Parsons. Mrs. Parsons and her husband, Fred, owned the Parsons Hotel in downtown Anchorage. Years after this photograph was taken, the sisters bought the hotel from the Parsons. Carlotta's granddaughter, Karen Cameron, today lives in Anchorage. *(Submitted by Karen Cameron)*

(ABOVE) ABOUT TO MAKE SOME SWEET MUSIC: The Metlakatla Band/Orchestra had talented, handsome performers when this photo was taken between 1915-1920. Missionary William Duncan was impressed by the musicality of the Tsimshian people, so he decided to further develop their talent. The instruments were a gift of a wealthy English silk manufacturer who was impressed by Duncan's work. Joel L. Baines Sr. learned the cornet and trombone for the brass band, the violin for the string orchestra. His son David of Anchorage says the Baines family had a strong affinity for music. Like their father, David and his brothers sang and played on many occasions. (*Submitted by David R. Baines*)

(ABOVE) A STORE TO REMEMBER: This is the interior of Brown and Hawkins' general merchandise store in Seward before 1910. Charles E. Brown and T.W. Hawkins were among Alaska's premier early merchants. The two apparently met in Nome, then moved to Valdez. In 1904, they set up shop in Seward. The firm sold everything - and everywhere in Alaska, with branches at Knik and Anchorage. The Brown and Hawkins Hall, completed in 1909, 80 feet long and 30 feet wide, was the scene of many dances and public gatherings. Brown and Hawkins, it can be truly said, did it all. *(Submitted by Iris and Hugh Darling)*

(RIGHT) THE RIVERS FAMILY: Julian Guy Rivers and his family are looking to please the photographer in the Dawson, Yukon Territory, of 1908. J.G., as some knew him, came to Alaska from Seattle in 1906 to work for the Guggenheim consortium. He brought his wife, Marie Louise, a little later. Marie Louise holds Lenora Zenaide. Behind them is Ralph and standing in front of J.G. is Victor. Once grown, Zenaide, as she was known, settled in California. Ralph became a lawyer - and the state's first congressman. Victor became an engineer - and member of the Alaska Legislature as well as a member of the Alaska Constitutional convention, authors of the state Constitution. He died in 1959. Upon his death, Gov. Bill Egan said "Many of the constructive enactments in our statute books came into being because of his vision and grasp of the needs of our vast area." *(Submitted by Julian Rivers)*

(LEFT) A WOMAN WITH A STORY: Elizabeth Kvasnikoff, born in 1872, holds Leland Shelford, her great-grandson. Elizabeth was a member of the Kvasnikoff family originally of Kodiak, later the first permanent residents of Ninilchik. In 1888, Elizabeth married gold miner Joseph Cooper, a Missouri man, for whom Cooper Landing is named. Elizabeth had nine children. After Joseph Cooper died, she married Steve Churkin, a Russian immigrant. Elizabeth is the great-grandmother of Lt. Gov. Loren Leman, elected with Gov. Frank Murkowski in 2002.
(Submitted by Wayne Leman)

THE ST. VALINTINE DOGRACE BALL. MOOSE HALL FLAT, ALASKA.   BASIL CLEMONS Photo. 1918.

(ABOVE) HAVING A BALL: Where else but Alaska would folks hold a "dog race ball?" This is the St. Valentine's Day Dog Race Ball in Flat, 1918. (Note "Valentine" is spelled incorrectly in the hand-written caption). Flat was a vibrant mining community near Iditarod. A visitor reported that Flat had a population of about 400 in 1910. That number decreased to 158 in the 1920 census. Perhaps close to half the town was in this photograph. *(Submitted by Julian Rivers)*

(RIGHT) VISITING THE BIG STUMP: A group of fishermen - names unknown - take a break next to a stump that must have been hard to climb. The scene is Seward, or near Seward, sometime before 1907. It's interesting that these folks seem to be wearing their Sunday best or something close to it. Did they catch any fish? The answer is lost to history. *(Submitted by Dorene Lorenz)*

(ABOVE) KEEPING TRACK OF THE GOODS: James J. Kelley, Seattle liquor merchant, sent this invoice with an order headed for Sitka. Commerce was a challenge in the early days. Goods moved slowly and merchants in Sitka and farther north had a tough time complaining to their suppliers in "the states." If the whiskey comes in a broken barrel, what can you do but scream? Thirsty customers were not appeased by assurances another barrel would be on the next ship - next month. Also, more than one merchant railed that he had been the victim of thieves who tapped the whiskey or beer barrel as it sat on a ship or dock. *(Submitted by John T. Jensen)*

Submitted by LaRue Hellenthal

Submitted by Frank M. Reed

(ABOVE) THE HOLIDAY ROADHOUSE: Residents of Wiseman in the Brooks Range gather for a holiday dinner in the late '20s. The occasion is unclear. What is clear is these holiday parties were inclusive. Everybody in the small community was invited. Feasting and dancing went on all night, into the next day. Robert Marshall, a brilliant New Yorker who lived in Wiseman in the late '20s and early 30's, thought Wiseman was Shangri-La, and celebrated the community in his widely praised book "Arctic Village." He said, "The real way to visit with the people of the Koyukuk is to visit the Wiseman roadhouse some evening at the end of supper time." True, but this photo tells us the roadhouse also was the right place to visit at the beginning of suppertime. *(Submitted by Michael Carey)*

(RIGHT) MARINERS UPON THE WATER ARE WE:
Members of the Sisters of Providence take to a lake near
Fairbanks, probably Harding Lake, in the summer of 1927. They
are, left to right: Sister Laurentin, Sister Marcien, Sister Pascal,
Sister Cresence, Provincial Superior Vincent Ferrier, Sister
Arcadius and Sister Yvonne Benoit. The provincial superior was
enjoying a little excursion when the photo was taken. She was in
Fairbanks to visit St. Joseph's Hospital. *(Submitted by Providence
Health System in Alaska)*

(LEFT) READY TO GO: Pilot A. A. Bennett
(second from right) has landed at Eagle in 1926 -
apparently on the Yukon River. Bennett was an
important figure in Interior aviation during the early
days, flying for the Bennett-Rodebaugh Co. The
company was formed in 1926 and sold to Alaskan
Airways Inc. in 1929. Bennett-Rodebaugh had four
aircraft operating out of Fairbanks when sold. Bennett
left Alaska in November 1929, relocating in Oregon
and later in Idaho. In 1967, a group of Anchorage
aviation enthusiasts and experts honored A. A. Bennett
as one of Alaska's 100 greatest bush pilots. *(Submitted by
Jim Hansen)*

(LEFT) RIGHT THIS WAY, MR. PRESIDENT:
President Warren Harding is on his way to the Anchorage
Hotel during his Alaska visit of 1923. His host was Frank I.
Reed, whose family owned the downtown hotel from 1916-
1935. The Reed family has been active in Alaska for more
than a hundred years. Frank I. came to Alaska from Iowa in
1900. He landed in Nome. President Harding was greeted
triumphantly everywhere he went in the territory. Tragically,
the Ohio Republican sickened and died soon after leaving
the Last Frontier. *(Submitted by Frank M. Reed)*

(RIGHT) TENTING ON THE CREEK: Chester Lloyd
Mayfield stands at the entrance of his tent, Cache Creek in the
Talkeetna region. It's 1921, and he is gold mining. This is pretty
much state of the art for camp life at the time. Note the wooden
base and wooden door frame. Also, a high stove pipe to keep
cinders away from the cloth. Tents like these were comfortable
enough, but in the dead of winter snow and cold presented
obvious problems. *(Submitted by Barbara Mayfield Kennedy)*

(ABOVE) A HAPPY FOURTH IN WASILLA: The town of Wasilla had only about 30 residents on Independence day 1927, but farmers and their families came to the local celebration. The building is Herning's Place (later Teeland's) on Main Street. The man sitting on the boardwalk may be Stanley Herning with his son Elmer. The boardwalk ran to the train station. *(Submitted by Wasilla-Knik Historical Society)*

(LEFT) AN ATTRACTIVE COUPLE AND CHILD: This photo is from the 1920s, which means outdoorsman and writer Charlie Mayse collected the photo but did not take it himself. Mayse was active along the Yukon River later than the '20s. Charlie says the two are Alec Peters and his wife, Julia. Alec seems to be an incredible dapper Dan as he looks confidently into the camera. Note the puttees on Alec's lower legs - a fashion statement not made in Alaska for a long, long time. *(Submitted by Charlie Mayse Collection)*

(RIGHT) BRINGING OUT THE BIG GUN: This float was part of a parade in downtown Anchorage, probably in 1917 or 1918, after the United States entered World War I. The gun represents "Big Bertha" the famed German cannon. The real "Big Bertha," weighed 43 tons and fired a 2,200-pound shell nine miles. It was named after the maker's wife - which gave her a measure of immortality she might not have taken as a compliment. The scene is Fourth Avenue and H Street. *(Submitted by Frank M. Reed)*

(ABOVE) THE PHOTO HAS A STORY: The Hernings, who owned the local store in Wasilla, (he is on the far left, she is in the middle holding coat) stand with a Mrs. Svenson (holding hat) and Eva and Gus Svenson (on the right). Johanna Olivia Frydenlund took the photo in the 20s. This photo and the other Frydenlund photos in the book have a remarkable story behind them. The Frydenlunds, Johanna, her husband Hans, and their children, returned to their native Norway in the '30s. Seventy years later their daughter, Betty Frydenlund (Bryne), who had been a child in Wasilla, came back. It was Betty's 50th wedding anniversary - and to celebrate she and members of the family visited. During their stay, Betty gave the photos to the Wasilla-Knik Historical Society. *(Submitted by Wasilla-Knik Historical Society)*

(ABOVE) PUTTING ON THE POWER: A construction crew pauses at Eklutna just north of Anchorage in 1928. They were building a power line from Eklutna to Anchorage. In 90 days, they completed 27.5 miles of line. Note the importance of the Alaska Railroad to the project. The men worked from the track as their base. Among the men in this picture are John Stewart (left), Leonard Berlin (third man) and Frank I. Reed (fifth of the six men). A rail station was established at the Native village of Eklutna in 1918. Eklutna had its own post office from 1926-1945. *(Submitted by Frank M. Reed)*

(LEFT) OUT FOR A PICNIC: Wasilla schoolchildren enjoy a picnic in 1926. They were attending the original Wasilla School. Johanna Olivia Frydenlund, whose daughter donated this photo and many others to the Wasilla-Knik Historical Society, took the photo. Some of the kids can be identified. On the far left, Bill Tryck. In the back center wearing a hat, Hilmer Oberg. On the right in back: Peter Snider. The Snider sisters are in front. With bow in hair: Pat Snider (Hjellen). To the right Marie Snider (Betts). Next to her, further right, is Ann Snider (Short). *(Submitted by Wasilla-Knik Historical Society)*

(RIGHT) A FLIGHT INTO THE RECORD BOOKS: Fairbanks Mayor Dr. F. de La Vergne hands pilot Noel Wien a letter for delivery in Nome, far away on the Bering Sea. The Fokker monoplane left Fairbanks June 5, 1925 and reached its destination 7 hours and 40 minutes later. The airplane revolutionized mail delivery. Before, it would have taken days for the letter to reach Nome. Conceivably, the writer of this letter could have received a reply the same day. *(Submitted by Bob Parrish)*

(LEFT) TAKE IT TO THE BANK: Banking played a crucial role in early Alaska - unless you kept your gold in a coffee can under the floorboards of your cabin. This bank book, belonging to Charles O'Halloran, was issued by the Miners and Merchants Bank of Iditarod in 1920. Iditarod, founded in 1910, had a population of 50 in 1920. And when O'Halloran made his first and only deposit in the bank on Sept. 28, 1920, he had a grand total of $600 in the Miners and Merchants vault. *(Submitted by Marilyn K. Patterson)*

(ABOVE) OUT ON THE BOARDWALK: Carmen Waldal Utt poses with her uncle Harold DeRoux on the boardwalk in Juneau/Douglas. It was 1928 and her two-week-old brother, Emil, was in the carriage. Harold spent 13 years in the US Coast Guard. Returning to civilian life he was general manager of the Juneau Federal Employees Credit Union. In later years, he ran boats in and around Valdez. Carmen attended business college in Seattle before returning to Alaska where she married a coal miner. The couple lived in the Mat-Su area. Emil worked at the Fort Richardson commissary for many years. He is retired and lives in the Mat-Su area. *(Submitted by Joann Utt)*

(RIGHT) A FAMILY SEARCHING FOR GOLD: The Swanberg family pauses for the camera on their mining ground near Nome. They are: Nels Swanberg Sr, Charlotte Swanberg, Nels Jr., Grace and Charlotte. Nels Sr. crossed the Chilkoot Pass in the days of '98 and met his wife Charlotte in Nome. They lived out their lives together in Nome. *(Submitted by Joy Berger)*

(RIGHT) MINING FOR AN EDUCATION: Rasmus Nielsen, Ralph Rivers, and Hans Galneck take a break from their search for gold in Flat, 1922. Ralph was a college student - from a mining family - who put himself through the University of Washington by mining in the summer. Born in 1903, Rivers had a distinguished career in Alaska public life. He was mayor of Fairbanks, territorial attorney general, a member of the territorial Legislature and the Constitutional Convention. He finished his public service career as the state's first congressman (1959-1966). He was by profession a lawyer and by choice a Democrat. *(Submitted by Julian Rivers)*

(ABOVE) GET OUT ON THE HIGHWAY: Hans F. Frydenlund tests a new vehicle on the streets of downtown Wasilla about 1925. Frydenlund, a Norwegian immigrant, hauled freight to the Independence Mine. He also owned the Willow Creek Inn, in the background. One wonders what ever happened to this creative piece of machinery and where it came from. Wasilla was a genuine frontier community when Frydenlund and his family lived there. Nobody zipped into Anchorage for the evening while Calvin Coolidge was president. *(Submitted by Wasilla-Knik Historical Society)*

Submitted by Jim Hansen

The 1930's

Submitted by James V. Elmore

Submitted by Karen Cameron

Submitted by James V. Elmore

(LEFT) HOME FOR A VISIT: College student Estella Irwin is home from college - probably at Easter - in the spring of 1934. The scene is the Agricultural Experiment Station in Matanuska. Don Irwin, Estella's father, was the director of the station. Estella married Louis Odsather - the first wedding at the log church in Palmer, Estella remembers. The couple had three children, two of whom live in Alaska while one lives in California. The Irwins came to Alaska from Wyoming. *(Submitted by Estella Odsather)*

(ABOVE) A VISITING CELEBRITY: Seward businessman Leon Urbach, right, and Will Rogers took a look around Southcentral Alaska in their trusty Ford sometime in the mid-'30s. Rogers, the cowboy philosopher, columnist, and lecturer, was one of the most celebrated figures of the day, beloved for his down home wisdom. He was proud of his Cherokee ancestry and often said "My ancestors may not have come over on the Mayflower, but they met 'em at the boat." Rogers and Wiley Post were killed in a plane crash near Barrow in 1935. Leon Urbach was a successful Seward businessman, who opened a general store, Urbach's, in 1915. *(Submitted by Dorothy Urbach)*

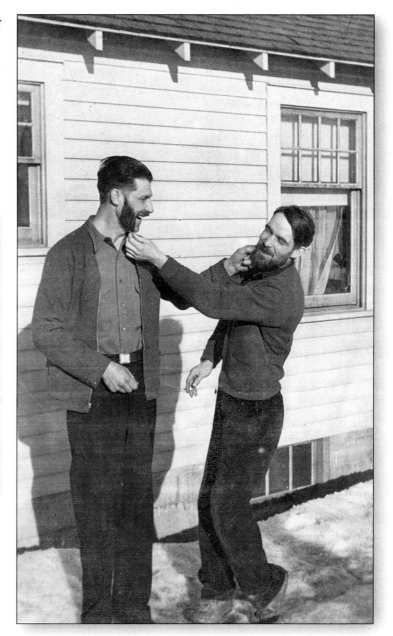

(RIGHT) CHECKING OUT THE FUR: A beard-growing contest has been part of the Anchorage Fur Rendezvous for a long time. In 1938, Dan Aylward was checking out the progress of George Renegard's beard on what looks like a warm day. A Norwegian immigrant, George was a carpenter and one of the founders of the first organized skiing activity in Anchorage. Dan was from Northfield, Minn. He first came to Alaska in 1935. Like many other Alaskans of his generation, he worked for the Alaska Railroad after settling in Anchorage. Dan eventually went into the construction business. He was vice president of O'Neill Construction Inc. at the time of his death in 1968 at the age of 59. *(Submitted by Alice White)*

(ABOVE) THE MASON'S SHAKE THINGS UP: Believe it or not, this is a Masonic meeting in Seward, sometime in the 1930s. The members apparently were putting on a little show. The Masonic Order was active in Alaska from the earliest days. Old newspapers are full of stories about Masonic "doings." Many obituaries mention the deceased's role in Masonic affairs. In Fairbanks, the Masonic Temple, built in 1906, is one of the community's oldest buildings. *(Submitted by Dorothy Urbach)*

(LEFT) GETTING THE BUGS OUT: "Captain Joe," Einar Johansen, is busy making ice cream and he is getting a little help. His daughter, Joann, is spraying "bug dope" to keep the mosquitoes away. Einar Johansen was a partner in the Grant Mining Co. on the Seward Peninsula, the Kougarok River country. The family mined in summer and lived in Nome, where they operated a lighterage business, the rest of the year. *(Submitted by Juli Braund-Allen)*

(RIGHT) THE LITTLEST MARINER: Joann Johansen christened a boat at Tony Jensen's shipyard on Lake Washington, Seattle, around 1930. Joann was the youngest of three sisters, daughters of miners Einar and Yetta Johansen of Nome. She eventually settled in the Chicago area and raised a family. Today, she lives in San Francisco. *(Submitted by Juli Braund-Allen)*

(RIGHT) WEDDING DAY: Carlton Washington Baldwin and his bride, Olinga Margaret Vaska, stand outside the Holy Cross Mission Church on their wedding day in 1934. Carlton came to Alaska from Minnesota in 1931. Olinga was born and raised in Piamute, Alaska. Carlton ran heavy equipment in mining camps, but for the most part the couple followed the subsistence life - hunting, fishing, trapping - in the Holy Cross, Bethel, Aniak area. *(Submitted by Joe Baldwin)*

(ABOVE) HAIL TO THE VICTORS: Curling has been popular in Alaska - and the Yukon Territory - for most of a hundred years. This team won the "Ham and Eggs Bonspiel" in the winter of 1931-1932. Members are, from left to right: John Dunn, Ralph Rivers, Jeff Studdart and Phil DeWree. Dunn, a Scotsman, was an engineer for Independent Lumber. Rivers went on to become the state's first congressman. Studdart had a long career in Fairbanks dog mushing. DeWree, from Belgium, ran a plumbing shop. Note: There also was a "Beef and Greens Bonspiel." Apparently, these bonspiels got their names from the menu at the dinner concluding the competition. *(Submitted by Julian Rivers)*

(LEFT) A TRIO OF SMILING YOUNGSTERS: The Kirsch boys, Jim, Ernie and Andy peer into the camera on a nice day in 1938. Their parents, John and Rose May, were Matanuska Valley colonists. Originally from North Dakota, they moved to Minnesota to qualify. The Kirsch family later had a lodge In Talkeetna. The lodge, Kirsch's place, was added to the National Register of Historic Places in 1998. The Kirsch story is a good example of how Matanuska Valley colonists adapted to Alaska. They lost their farm to foreclosure and moved on to build the lodge. *(Submitted by Paul Roseland)*

(ABOVE) BREAKUP IN FAIRBANKS: These two kids were on the beach - such as it was - of the Chena River sometime in the early '30s. Breakup was a major event back then. Not only did it signal the end of winter, downtown Fairbanks might (and sometimes did) flood. The large vessel on the left is the Idler, which plied the Chena, Tanana and Yukon rivers. A happy day it was in the villages when the Idler was back on the water - summer supplies were on their way. *(Submitted by The Bruce Haldeman Collection)*

(RIGHT) A CAREFUL LOOK: Anton Anderson, left, and Roy McDonald, right, scope out a proposed landing site for floatplanes. Anderson - the city engineer - was also at one time the mayor of Anchorage. McDonald was chairman of the Aeronautic Commission. It's 1934, and the men are meeting at the Anchorage Airport (Merrill Field). Clearly, the people of Anchorage have had big dreams about aviation for a long, long time. *(Submitted by Jean Graves)*

(BELOW) DANCING THE NIGHT AWAY: The 1930 Anchorage Chamber of Commerce Ball must have been quite the event judging from this dance card. Most folks today have never even seen a dance card, but back when Paul Whiteman was the nation's great bandleader, the belle of the ball needed to keep track of her partners. The belle in this case was Louise Gill (Moore), age 18. (Louise moved to Seattle in the '40s.) Note the dance names, especially the "Piggly Wiggly" Wiggle. The Wiggle - and other dance names - were probably cute allusions to local businesses. *(Submitted by Christine Gill)*

Anchorage Chamber of Commerce

ANNUAL BALL

and

Merchants' Exposition

ANCHORAGE, ALASKA
"The Biggest Little City in the World"

ELKS' BALL ROOM
May 17, 1930

(ABOVE) THE FACE OF LAW AND KAY: Some people would call this a rose between two thorns. On this day in the '30s, the woman in the middle is writer Kay Kennedy. Kay was a roving reporter for many Alaska publications. On the left is Jack O'Connor, senior game warden in the territory of Alaska. Jack was known as an honest man. "Why that guy would arrest his own grandmother," a sourdough told Kay. Sam White, on the right, looks a little offbeat in a tie. He was a game warden, also, eventually better known than O'Connor. When asked by a kid (Michael Carey), how to deter lawbreakers, Sam said, "Build lots of jails, sonny, and fill 'em." Sam was Alaska's first flying game warden - and flew an open cockpit ship at 40 below. *(Submitted by Charlie Mayse Collection)*

ABOVE) OFF TO THE RACES: This is a classic Fairbanks dog-mushing scene from the late 1930s. The race is about to begin, much of the town has gathered. Many fans are looking down on the Chena River from the old Cushman Saint bridge. Races often were held over several days on a course that looped through and round the community. In those days, the mushers were all Alaskan - it would take too long for a stateside musher to get to Fairbanks for the competition. *(Submitted by The Bruce Haldeman Collection)*

(ABOVE) THERE'S A STORY HERE: This is a mining camp in Flat, near Iditarod, probably in the late '30s or early '40s. The man with the hat sitting on the truck (middle back) is George Mathieson. George, born 1890, was a Scottish immigrant who came to Alaska in the early days the hard way - he mushed from the "states." It took him three months. George and his brothers, Hugh and Alex, entered the mining game and had a large, successful operation in Flat. *(Submitted by Kathy Campbell)*

(RIGHT) REAL ALASKANS: Ernest and Olga Peck, shown here near Wasilla, were married Jan. 22, 1920, at Pilot Station on the Yukon River. For a while Ernest co-owned a trading post on Bristol Bay. The couple later went up the Yukon to Galena and Kaltag, where Ernest taught school. In the early '30s, they moved to Wasilla, homesteading on Lake Lucille. On Aug. 1, 1970, the Anchorage Times noted that Ernest and Olga invited family and friends to their home to celebrate their 50th wedding anniversary. Peck Street in Wasilla was named for them. *(Submitted by Wasilla-Knik Historical Society)*

(BELOW) SAILORS ROLLING: Three sailors stand in front of Pat's Cafe, near Dutch Harbor, in 1938. Milton S. Collins, also a sailor, took the photo. Collins was in the Navy for 30 years. He settled in California - never having ventured beyond coastal Alaska to the Interior or other parts of the territory/state. *(Submitted by Kellie Compelube)*

(LEFT) A COUPLE WITH A STORY: Walt and Vivian Teeland made their name virtually synonymous with Wasilla - as in Teeland's store. Walt was born near Fairbanks in 1907. He worked in general stores as a boy, later for the old road commission, and had his own trucking company, Walt's Transfer. He also worked for the Alaska Railroad. Vivian was the daughter of well-known coal miner Evan Jones. In 1947, the two, who married in 1933, purchased a Wasilla business that became Teeland's Country Store. Walt and Vivian ran the store until 1972. The store still stands after having been refurbished by the Wasilla-Knik Historical Society and friends. *(Submitted by Wasilla-Knik Historical Society)*

(RIGHT) FISHING WITH FRIENDS: The boys pose with a good catch at Fish Creek, near Nenana, in 1937 or 1938. Left to right they are Jack Coghill, Bob Coghill, Fred Hupprich, Bob Hupprich and George Hupprich. The Coghills and Hupprichs were well known in the Interior - still are. Brother Bill Coghill took the photo. Jack Coghill has been active in civic affairs for nearly half a century. He was a member of the Alaska Constitutional Convention as well as lieutenant governor of Alaska. *(Submitted by Bill Coghill)*

(ABOVE) A MINER'S MINER: George Mathieson, miner, takes a break from the day's labors sometime in the '30s. George and his two brothers mined successfully at Flat for many years from the '20s on. The family, like many mining families, wintered in "the states." George's two children grew up in Oakland. Los Angeles was George's final home. He lived to be 100. Kathy Campbell, George's granddaughter, resides in Anchorage. She says that of George two children and seven grandchildren only she has been to Alaska for more than a week. *(Submitted by Kathy Campbell)*

(ABOVE) THE WHOLE SCHOOL WAS THERE: Alaska had only about 65,000 people when this photograph was taken at Ninilchik in 1935. Many schools were small if not outright tiny. By the standards of the day, the Ninilchik Territorial School was a pretty good size. The students are: Back Row: Joe Leman, Abraham Kvasnikoff, Peter Cooper, Margaret Jackinosky, Fedora Kvasnikoff, John Matson. Middle Row: Mike Kvasnikoff, David Cooper, Robert Cooper, Frank Cooper Jr., Harry Leman, Cara Jackinosky and Ella Oskolkoff. Front Row: Donald Oskolkoff, Larry Oskolkoff, Lawrence Matson, Ann Leman, Sophie Cooper, Irene Kvasnikoff, Gladys Steik, Susie Kvasnikoff, Alice Oskolkoff and Martin Cooper. *(Submitted by Loren Leman)*

(LEFT) A DAY AT THE BEACH, ANCHORAGE STYLE: Swimmers and friends enjoy some warm weather on Lake Spenard around 1938-1940. Note structure in background - where folks gathered if the weather turned wet. The people are unidentified except for the woman on the left, Sidonia (Martens) Gill, wife of Vic Gill, owner of Gill's Garage in downtown Anchorage. *(Submitted by Christine Gill)*

(RIGHT) COMPETING IN THE CARNIVAL: The 1935 Anchorage hockey team stands on the ice of the Chena River, Fairbanks. The team was competing in the Fairbanks Ice Carnival. Today, it's difficult to realize just how important the carnival was to Alaskans. People from all over the territory came for the activities and a good time. Among others in the photo are "Andy" Anderson, "Swede" Larson, Hank Schroeder, Asa Martin, Vern Johnson, Tom Cullhane, Bill Pascoe and Herb Schroeder. *(Submitted by UAA Blueliners/Brian McKay)*

(LEFT) RUB-A-DUB-DUB: Jack and Margaret Lindsey (now Anderson) are comfortable in their Rinso box on the Seward boardwalk around 1936. Jack followed in his father's footsteps and joined the Alaska Railroad. During World War II, the railroad was short of men and put Jack to work as a 14-year-old fireman. Jack had a long career with the railroad, becoming the Fairbanks facility manager. He died in 1994. Margaret still lives in Seward. *(Submitted by Margaret Lindsey Anderson)*

(LEFT) THE SEWARD KIDS: Margaret, Jack and Dale Lindsey looked the camera in the eye in 1939. Father Ed Lindsey had come to Alaska in 1923 to work on the Alaska Railroad. He was living in Wyoming at the time and responded to an ad the railroad published when it was looking for a few good men. Later, he brought his wife, Eva. Ed retired from the railroad after a lengthy career. Dale is a Seward businessman, owner of Harbor Enterprises. *(Submitted by Margaret Lindsey Anderson)*

(ABOVE) A VALUABLE CRITTER: A silver fox is penned on a fox farm, Skilak Lake, the Kenai Peninsula, about 1930. silver fox was all the rage in high society before the Great Depression, and many Alaskans tried raising the animals for profit. Some were successful, some not. But the big money did not come easy. Many farmers knew little or nothing about fox. According to Fur Fish Game magazine, fur buyers in 1928 were paying as much as $350 for a Number One Large silver fox . Top-grade medium-sized silver fox brought $225. Good money today - even better money when Calvin Coolidge was president. *(Submitted by Henry Kaiser Jr.)*

(LEFT) OUT WITH THE FAMILY: Ferb and Ruth Bailey and their children enjoy a picnic at Hatcher Pass north of Anchorage. Note snow in background. Ferb was a farmer who lived on Bailey Hill near Palmer. This photo was taken in 1936. Ferb enjoyed Alaska but eventually decided he had had enough. He moved back to Wisconsin, leaving many friends behind. *(Submitted by Dorothy Butch)*

(RIGHT) THE DIGGING WENT ON FOR YEARS: Biner Wind (left) and R. H. Creecy (right) were miners in the Wiseman area. This photo was probably taken at their diggings on the Hammond River in the 1920s or 1930s. Creecy was a black Spanish-American War veteran who came north to mine and spent the rest of his life on the creeks. He may have been from Virginia or Georgia. The 1920 and 1930 censuses disagree. After years in the Bush, Creecy visited Fairbanks for medical treatment and told the local newspaper he had just seen automobiles for the first time. He also marveled at the beauty and "modern" attire of the women of the Golden Heart City, telling the paper "I never before saw women that look like these women." Creecy died near Wiseman in late 1948 or early 1949. He was buried Jan. 22, 1949. *(Submitted by George Lounsbury)*

(LEFT) A BIT OF CIVIC HIGH JINKS: A local ladies homemakers' club in Palmer was singing "Home on the Range," or at least something similar, when this photo was taken in front of the Palmer school in 1937. Members of the group include Irene Beylund, Grace Anderson, Alice Sjodin, Lulubelle Bowens, Irene Benson (holding guitar), ? Becktle, Marge Hoskins and Lillian Eckert. Check the "shoes" the horse is sporting. Unfortunately, the identity of the "horseplayers" is not known - nor that of the small girl and the small boy. *(Submitted by Dorothy Butch)*

(BELOW) THEY WERE ALL SMILES: Midge Reeve (Andresen) and friends put their skis down long enough for this photo, taken on a ski trip near Fairbanks in 1936. Midge, the woman on the left, went on to marry Clark Andresen, a successful salesman who traveled Alaska on business for more than 40 years. The couple retired to Seattle in 1976. Midge now lives in Anchorage. The young man on the right is probably George Karabelnikof who also lives in Anchorage. *(Submitted by Midge Andresen)*

(LEFT) A REAL TRAPPER: George McIsaac is packing his pelts home after a successful trapping venture. McIsaac was born in Seattle, grew up in Anchorage where his parents owned the Hotel Seattle. His mother, a relative says, was a bootlegger who delivered the product in her baby carriage. George McIsaac lived in Anchorage from the '20s through the '50s and spent many a winter on snowshoes working his lines. He eventually moved back to Washington state, settling in the town of Quincy. *(Submitted by Donna Linburgh)*

(RIGHT) WHO THEY ARE REMAINS UNKNOWN: Sailor Milton S. Collins took this photo near Dutch Harbor while he was passing through. Perhaps someone will recognize who the three are as Collins did not take notes. Collins' photos of Alaska - and his stories - so impressed his daughter, Kellie Compelube, that she came to Alaska to satisfy her "curiosity." Eventually, she and her husband, Steve, settled in Anchorage. Kellie says she likes Alaska so much she is never going back to the Lower 48. Photographs really can change lives. *(Submitted by Kellie Compelube)*

(ABOVE) A MOST TASTY MORSEL: Robert Weimer feeds a fox he has befriended at Denali National Park. Weimer came to Alaska from Johnstown, PA in 1929. He intended to make enough money to start a business in his home state but instead made Alaska his home. When this photo was taken, 1930 or '31, Weimer was building the road into Denali. He was a blaster. *(Submitted by Bonnie Tisler)*

(LEFT) STRIKE UP THE BAND: A Native band gathers for a group photograph in Sitka. The locale is certain as John Jensen inherited the photo from his father, who lived in Sitka. Note the diverse ages of the bandsmen. Bands like this were important community institutions and especially prominent on major holidays. Recognize any of these well turned out fellows? *(Submitted by John T. Jensen)*

(RIGHT) NEITHER SLEET NOR SNOW - NOR FLOATING ICE: Adolph Biederman and his son, Horace, carry the mail across the Yukon River on Oct. 29, 1934. Note that there were eight dogs in the boat, although only one is easily visible. Adolph, an immigrant from Bavaria, packed the mail from Eagle to Circle for many years. Ultimately, the airplane put him out of business; it was so much swifter than a dog team. Horace Biederman later operated a store in Eagle. Old-timers like the Biedermans were accustomed to hard work and difficult conditions, as this photograph demonstrates.

(Submitted by Jim Hansen)

(RIGHT) WEARING THE TRADITIONAL GARB: The Rev. Ludwig Ost wears a seal-gut parka in Elim, 1915. The parka was new. He went on whaling excursions between Alaska and Siberia in this garb. Ost came to Alaska in 1910, a missionary for the Swedish Covenant Church. Over the years, Ost played many important roles in Seward Peninsula communities. *(Submitted by Gail Phillips)*

(ABOVE) A WINDOW ON THE BABY SHOP: The Baby Shop, 433 4th Avenue Anchorage, is a busy place on this day in 1939. Edith Waldron, the owner, is in the background to the right. Evelyn Torpa, Edith's niece, is behind the counter. The customer at the counter is Lorraine-Saxton Waldron, with the smiling baby in The Baby Shop, Billie Grace Waldron. The shop was in business for more than 20 years. Its slogan was "necessities for the new boss". *(Submitted by Art L. "Bill" Waldron)*

(LEFT) HERE COMES THE POTATO MAN: Lawrence Vasanoja stands by Jalmar Wineck's truck in the Matanuska Valley. Lawrence had 12 acres where he grew potatoes, like those bagged on the truck. To harvest the potatoes, Lawrence hired the wives of Matanuska "colonists" to pick the potatoes. They in turn received free spuds for a year. *(Submitted by Pearl M. Jensen)*

(RIGHT) REAL CONTRIBUTORS TO THIER COMMUNITY: Lillian Phillips (left) stands with Becky Joy and her son, Jimmy, 1935-1936. At the time, Lillian, a registered nurse, provided the only medical service between Chitna and Nebesna in the Copper River area. The work she began culminated in the Glennallen clinic. Lillian came to Alaska with Becky and Vincent Joy, who founded the Central Alaska Mission. *(Submitted by Walt Phillips Jr.)*

(RIGHT) HEADING FOR THE MINE: Barney, "Ole" (Borghild) and their son Jim, all Hansens, are on their way out of Eagle to their family mine. The Hansens mined in the region for nearly 40 years. "Ole" was a teacher in Eagle before marrying. The Hansens built their own sleds, like this one, to carry their supplies and material. Eagle is one of the older cities in Interior Alaska. As early as the 1870s, there was a trading post at the location that became the city of Eagle. *(Submitted by Jim Hansen)*

(LEFT) THEY KEPT TRACK OF THE TRAIL: Walter Phillips and his dog, Red, had a big job. Winter and summer, they patrolled the first 60 miles of the telegraph line out of Valdez to ensure it was in working order. In winter, Walter traveled on skis and snowshoes. In summer, he drove a Model A truck. Driving sounds easier than skiing - except that the roads of yesteryear were subject to serious washouts. Walter had this job from the late '30s into World War II. *(Submitted by Walt Phillips Jr.)*

Submitted by Elvi Rebarcheck

The 1940's

Submitted by Karen Cameron

Submitted by Karen Cameron

Submitted by Mary Moran

(LEFT) MISS ALASKA AND CLASSIC SCENE: Minnie Motschman, Miss Alaska 1940, is on the runway in Fairbanks - Weeks Field - with two modes of transportation. Chambers of commerce, postcard makers and apparently the general public loved scenes like this in which the "old" stood in immediate contrast to the "new." Minnie was one of Richard and Mary Motschman's ten children. *(Submitted by Marie Motschman)*

(RIGHT) HAPPY TO BE HOME AT LAST: Bob and Shirley Horrell were married two days before Bob shipped overseas during World War II. They were not reunited for two years. They are together at last in this photo from after the war. Bob and Shirley started the H and D Market in Anchorage in 1946. They had other businesses as well over a long and successful career. The couple still lives in Anchorage as does one of their four children, Don. Shirley still has a green thumb and remains an outstanding gardener. Alaska was a land of opportunity for Bob and Shirley Horrell and they made the most of it. *(Submitted by Joyce Horrell)*

(ABOVE) A FISH STORY AND MORE: John Stockhausen holds his catch as daughters Darlene and Nancy look on. John built the cabin in the background in 1947. It was on a homestead in the Peter's Creek area. The family came to Alaska from Wisconsin and eventually patented the homestead. Darlene still lives in Alaska in Chugiak. *(Submitted by Darlene Halverson)*

(LEFT) HANGING ON FOR DEAR LIFE: Carolyn Johnson is hanging around having fun over the table at the family mining camp. Carolyn was born in 1939 and has lived in Alaska all her life. Her three children and five grandchildren live here, too. Her father, Karl Butkovich, had the Fern Mine in Hatcher Pass, near the Independence Mine. The mine is long closed. *(Submitted by Carolyn Johnson)*

(ABOVE) SERVING ONLY THE BEST: Leo Michalek prepares to make a run in the Shamrock Bakery truck, probably in Palmer. He was one of four owners of the Matanuska Valley bakery, a popular place. Bakeries were important business institutions from the earliest days. Fresh bread was a luxury to miners in the old gold camps. More than one miner who didn't find gold, but could cook, found some pay dirt in a bakery. *(Submitted by Mary Ann Anderson)*

(RIGHT) **CATCHING THE BIG FISH:** Drusilla Kendrick and prize catch pause for the camera in 1947. They are on the family farm in the Butte area near Palmer. The family fished, appropriately enough, at Fish Creek - and put up the catch for the winter. Drusilla still lives in Palmer, but her daughter Lois says she doesn't fish as much any more. *(Submitted by Lois Kendrick)*

(LEFT) PALMER WAS THEIR HOME: Dorothy and Louis Henke stand with their daughter, Sharon, in Palmer about 1944. Louis drove a milk truck and raised potatoes, although he was a civil engineer by profession. The family moved to Kenai in 1950 and Louis resumed engineering. From the mid-'50s until the early '60s, the Henkes lived in Anchorage. They left Alaska in May 1961. *(Submitted by Michele MacIntyre)*

(ABOVE) BUSINESS WAS HUMMING RIGHT ALONG: This is the inside of the Shamrock Bakery in Palmer in 1947 or 1948. Leo Michalek, Matt Perkins, Harry Rice and Everett Pederson owned the bakery. Mary Ann Anderson, Leo's daughter, says Matt Perkins went on to found the Perkins Family Restaurant chain, which has more than 475 outlets in 35 states. Burt Parker, pictured on the right, was legally blind and made all the sweet rolls by touch. The old-time bakery is mighty inviting. *(Submitted by Mary Ann Anderson)*

(RIGHT) COOKING FOR PROVIDENCE: The Sourdough Cook Book was published in 1940 as a fund raiser for the "new" Providence Hospital. Anchorage residents submitted most of the recipes, but there also were recipes from as far away as Fairbanks and Juneau. In keeping with the times, married women, at least most of them, were identified by their husbands' names. As in Mrs. Fred M. Johnson (Scalloped Salmon and Vegetables) and Mrs. Frank O'Donnell (Salmon cakes). Dick Tousley, a trapper, offered a recipe for Boiled Moose Tongue. As follows: 4 chili capinis, 3 bay leaves, salt. Boil tongue slowly for several hours. Peel when done. Serve with horseradish and sourdough biscuits. *(Submitted by Dave Miller)*

(ABOVE) FOR HE'S A JOLLY GOOD FELLOW: The man on the right looks like a Charles Dickens character lost in Fairbanks as he poses with an unidentified soldier (middle) and Rolf Wittmer on the left. The time is probably the eve of World War II. Rolf Wittmer came to Alaska in 1940, when military construction was beginning to boom. He spent many years working at Elmendorf and retired as chief of the structures branch of the 21st Civil Engineering Squadron. When the photo was taken, Rolf was working at Ladd Field in Fairbanks (now Fort Wainwright). *(Submitted by Philippa Wittmer Paige)*

SOURDOUGH COOK BOOK

ALASKAN RECIPES BY ALASKA'S BEST COOKS

(LEFT) THE WHOLE CREW ASSEMBLED:
Cannery workers at the Portlock cannery, east of English Bay and Port Graham, were a busy bunch when this photo was taken in 1945. The war inevitably produced a labor shortage while stimulating demand for salmon. Some of the workers have been identified: second from left, Jerry Thompson; third from left, Martha Thompson. The tall man in the back is J.N. Thompson. *(Submitted by Greta Eidem)*

(RIGHT) YOU HAD TO HAVE PERMISSION: During World War II, civilians needed the military's permission to enter Alaska. After the attack on Dutch Harbor, the territory was a combat zone. No unneeded civilians wanted. The application for a permit to enter Alaska was quite detailed, requiring all kinds of information about the applicant's history and purpose in coming to Alaska. After review, a ranking officer signed it. This is Lorraine Martens' permit. Note that she was a clerk at the Alaska Railroad. Lorraine was from Iowa. She came to Alaska in the '30s. She was eventually joined in Anchorage by seven siblings. All eight found a home in the community. *(Submitted by Christine Gill)*

(RIGHT) FOLLOW HAROLD'S RULES: Helen Jewett and her daughter, Charleen Gallagher Bentson, stand in front of Harold's Place, Ketchikan. Helen worked there for owner Harold Blanton. Harold must have been a man with a sense of humor. He printed a pamphlet on bar room etiquette that cleverly turned good behavior upside down. For example, Harold wrote, "If the bartender is busy at the end of the bar, clap loudly with your hands or hammer the polished surface with a coin or glass. Better still, whistle or call... 'Hey you' or 'Hey bartender'." Apparently Harold had seen his share of customers who had not read Emily Post. *(Submitted by Charleen Gallagher Bentson)*

(BELOW) FIRST COMMUNION: A classic scene in Anchorage in front of Family Catholic Church at Fifth and H Street. It's 1942 or '43 and first communion for Jack Aylward, the finely turned out youngster in the front middle, looking down. Danny Aylward, his brother, is the altar boy on the right standing

in front of The Rev. Dermot O'Flanigan. Danny went on to a career in construction work in Anchorage. Little Jack grew up and went away. He received an electrical engineering degree from the University of Washington and lives in Seattle. O'Flanigan arrived in Anchorage in 1935 and became bishop of Juneau in 1951. *(Submitted by Alice White)*

HAROLD'S PLACE

Cocktail Bar and Liquor Store

Ketchikan, Alaska

(LEFT) BRINGING IN THE HARVEST: Young Bill Wimmer gives a hand to the potato harvest in Palmer, 1942. His mother, Lucille, looks on. Lucille's husband, Harry Wimmer, came to Alaska from Kansas in 1934. He was for many years, the high school principal in Palmer. Later, he was an elementary school principal in Anchorage. Lucille lives in Anchorage. Bill lives in Arizona. *(Submitted by Robert and Joan Wimmer)*

(RIGHT) A LITTLE NIGHT MUSIC: An unknown accordion player performs for south central Alaska listeners over KFQD radio in 1941. The controller in the background is William J. Barber. KFQD recruited Barber out of Portland, Oregon. He worked in a radio parts store. The owner knew people at KFQD. Barber maintained the KFQD transmitter and operated the controls for the record player. His wife, Jessie, was an announcer at the station. In 1942, Barber went to work for the federal agency that would become the FAA. He worked for them for 30 years, serving all over Alaska as a electronics technician and station manager. *(Submitted by William J. Barber)*

(ABOVE) THERE FOR A VISIT: Ethel Rich came to visit her children at the Matanuska Valley Children's home this day in 1947. The children were in the home because their parents, Ethel and Tom, worked and lived on Fort Richardson. Regulations prevented the children from staying with their parents. The couple visited every weekend. Ethel is standing in the back. In front of her are Joanna, Janice, Tommy and David Rich. Tom took the photograph. *(Submitted by Jan Johnson)*

(LEFT) AN OLD BUT IMPORTANT THEME: Buy Alaska! is the word at this unnamed Anchorage store near the end of World War II. It's a theme that still resonates. Note the variety of Alaska products. Alaska producers always have faced tough competition from Outside. If stateside merchants endured the proverbial "freight," Alaska businesses were hampered by what the locals called the "HCL" - the "high cost of living," including operating costs far above those in "the states." Wonder who produced the "Bleach From Anchorage"? *(Submitted by Bob Parrish)*

(RIGHT) A TEAM TO REMEMBER: The Sheldon Jackson Junior College women's team of 1948 in a photo taken by Luella Smith of the Sitka Photo Shop. Basketball was immensely popular in southeast Alaska, spawning many rivalries. The players are, top left, Alice Moy and, top right, Barbara Hamilton. Second row: Mary Baines, Merna Gardner, Nina Cook and Alma Nelson. Third row: Marie Johnson and Annabelle Phillips. Adelaide Bartness is holding the ball. The team's big rival was Sitka High School. *(Submitted by David R. Baines)*

(RIGHT) ED TAKES A BREAK: It's time for coffee on Ed Touissant's boat as he motors along the Yukon River toward Fort Yukon. Ed was better known as a pilot, operator of Touissant's Flying Service. In the '40s, he flew in and out of Fort Yukon to nearby communities and Fairbanks. C. Masten Beaver, who knew Ed, describes him as "a solid, chunky young man, in his early thirties, built along the lines of a heavyweight prize fighter, with curly, unruly brown hair and a broad, determined face that wore a perpetual happy grin." *(Submitted by Charlie Mayse Collection)*

(ABOVE) THE GENERAL AND THE QUEEN: Gen. Simon Bolivar Buckner Jr., commanding general of Alaska during World War II, and Patricia Chisholm, the Fur Rendezvous queen, enjoy a laugh sometime during the war years. The gentleman on the right is unidentified. Gen. Buckner, who liked to be called "The Silver Stallion of Alaska," oversaw the buildup of the military in Alaska and the combat operations that followed. He was killed in the spring of 1945 at Okinawa. Patricia Chisholm, who came from a prominent Anchorage business family, went on to marry an officer. *(Submitted by Karen Cameron)*

(LEFT) CHECKING OUT THE ACTION: Rolf Wittmer, bearded man left of center, checks out a card game (blackjack?) in Fairbanks, probably 1940. The crowd may be so big - and so open - because the game of chance was part of the Fairbanks Winter Carnival. Rolf settled in Anchorage and worked at Elmendorf for many years, receiving the Air Force Medal for Meritorious Civilian Service. Two of his three children live in Alaska. *(Submitted by Philippa Wittmer Paige)*

(RIGHT) A BOAT OF HIS OWN: Werner Munk was stationed in Adak in 1947-48. He built this boat himself out of 3/4-inch plywood and two by fours. The wood came from a Quonset hut, which the Army was preparing to tear down. "The design fit what I had," Munk said. Munk put a two-cycle inboard engine in the boat, and then tried to circumnavigate the island with a 55-gallon drum of gas to fuel the engine. He burned so much gas so quickly he decided he'd better quit the voyage and head for home port. *(Submitted by Werner Munk)*

(BELOW) A FRIENDLY FOX: Werner Munk pulled this fox out of a den - and adopted it. Munk is standing in front of a Quonset hut on Adak. He lived in one of the huts in 1947- '48. Munk brought the fox to camp, but after a week, the brass told him the guest would have to go. Munk left Alaska. It was more than two decades - 1973 - before he returned for a visit. In 1974, he settled here, taking an engineering job during construction of the trans-Alaska pipeline. He still lives in Anchorage. *(Submitted by Werner Munk)*

(ABOVE) THEY WERE BUILDING THE BASE: Construction workers at Fort Richardson take a brief break, sometime in 1947. The men were part of a large group of workers busily employed on military projects in the Anchorage area. In 1940, there were only 1,000 military personnel in the entire territory. By 1947, that figure had grown to 25,000. Hence the many military projects. Tom Rich, an oiler, is third from the left. His wife, Ethel, worked in the mess hall. *(Submitted by Jan Johnson)*

(ABOVE) DREAM A LITTLE DREAM: Fourteen-year-old Betty Boyd Leman (Schneiter) sits on the porch of John Matson's home in Ninilchik, the summer of 1945. Betty says, "In those days it was THE thing for girls to have some military preference and the Navy was mine. I don't know where I got the hat, but I wore it a lot! I was going to join the WAVES as soon as I was old enough, but about two months after this picture was taken, World War II ended." Betty now lives in Philomath, OR. *(Submitted by Stephanie Leman)*

(ABOVE) THEY WERE HEADED NORTH: The Alaska Steamship Co's Columbia left Seattle for Ketchikan June 22, 1940, and passengers were handed this list of their fellow voyagers. "Knowing your fellow travelers," wrote the company in the introduction, "will add much to the pleasure of your voyage...." The list was broken into "Round Trip Passengers" and passengers for Ketchikan and Seldovia. The term "round tripper" was old Alaskan for "tourist" but presumably some of these "round trippers" were business travelers. This little booklet suggests an era when travel was elegant, when travel was infrequent if not rare and to be treasured in memory *(Submitted by Christine Gill)*

(ABOVE) THE FLIERS ARE BACK: Pilots, their girls and their friends gather at a Spokane, WA field in March 1942. The first man on the left is Carl Garver. Next to him on the right is Patricia Chisholm. John Murphy is the next man to the right. The rest are unidentified. A note on the photo says "12 fighter pilots had been flown to the U.S. from the Aleutian Islands to pick up new fighter planes." Patricia Chisholm, from Anchorage, was a student at Stevens College (Missouri) at the time. Patricia's father, Jack, was a prominent Anchorage salesman and merchant, known all over the territory. *(Submitted by Karen Cameron)*

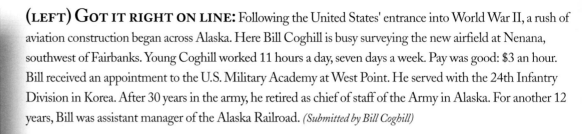

(LEFT) GOT IT RIGHT ON LINE: Following the United States' entrance into World War II, a rush of aviation construction began across Alaska. Here Bill Coghill is busy surveying the new airfield at Nenana, southwest of Fairbanks. Young Coghill worked 11 hours a day, seven days a week. Pay was good: $3 an hour. Bill received an appointment to the U.S. Military Academy at West Point. He served with the 24th Infantry Division in Korea. After 30 years in the army, he retired as chief of staff of the Army in Alaska. For another 12 years, Bill was assistant manager of the Alaska Railroad. *(Submitted by Bill Coghill)*

(LEFT) WRITING IN THE SUN: Wendy Jones sits comfortably on the front porch of her cabin on Jones Lake in West Anchorage, near the airport. Wendy and her husband, Glen, homesteaded the area, starting in 1948. Wendy is working on the manuscript of "Trudy the Trailer," a story of her travels in Florida. The book was published in 1951. Glen still lives on the corner of Jones Avenue and Wendy's Way in the Glen Park Estates subdivision. *(Submitted by Bob Parrish)*

(RIGHT) ON THE WAY TO FAIRBANKS: Lu-Dean and Doyle Boatwright were on their way to Fairbanks in 1940. Back then, the trip was not a one-day affair given the condition of the roads. The Boatwright children traveled with their mother, who was joining their father, a construction worker, in the Golden Heart City. The Boatwrights settled in Seward in 1943. Note the dog. Lu-Dean says the hound had a bell around his neck. He would "ring" the bell in the morning, notifying guests that it was time for breakfast. *(Submitted by Lu-Dean Knight)*

(ABOVE) HERE COMES THE PARADE: A large throng has gathered in downtown Anchorage for the 1947 Fourth of July parade. The photo was taken somewhere near the old city hall. Note the sign for the 515 Club. The club remains in business more than 56 years later. Holiday parades were especially important in earlier days because they brought the community together and provided a sense of continuity and history. Remember, Anchorage was barely 40 years old when this photograph was taken. *(Submitted by Bernard and Daisy Swaboda)*

(LEFT) ONE GREAT LEAD DOG: This is Butch, Fabian Carey's lead dog. Fabian, father of editor Michael Carey, trapped for many years in the Lake Minchumina area and handsome Butch led the rest of Carey's dogs. Butch traveled hundreds of miles every year in weather far below zero and in temperatures above freezing, when he was panting and ready to quit. He never did. Butch was drafted in World War II - when Fabian was drafted, the dogs came with him - and served in the Alaska Scouts. Butch led scouting missions on the Alaska Peninsula at the end of the war. A great dog - he served his master, he served his country. *(Submitted by Michael Carey)*

(ABOVE) ON YOUR MARK, GET SET...: Runners assemble for the 1944 Mount Marathon race in Seward. Note the absence of modern running clothes. Runners ran for the mountaintop in what they had handy - trunks and sneakers at best. Seward was a busy community in 1944, especially because of World War II. Soldiers like the man in uniform to the left would have been a common sight. Who won? Unfortunately, we don't know. *(Submitted by Lu-Dean Knight)*

(RIGHT) TAKING A BIG JUMP: Henrietta Swanson Lee took this photograph of a ski jumper known only as "Loyd" on Feb. 29, 1948. The jump scaffolding was near the old Alaska Native hospital in downtown Anchorage. Henrietta wrote "a great leap year day". Here Loyd is going to take an extra jump and among the watchers you will find Mae, the Baxters and Burch." A nice moment - but who these people were, except Henrietta, has been lost. She was the sister of postmaster Paul Swanson of Chugiak. *(Submitted by Chugiak-Eagle River Historical Society)*

(LEFT) SHARING CHRISTMAS CHEER: It's Christmas Day 1949 in the Matanuska Valley and friends and neighbors have gathered at the Henry Hanson home. The group includes Paul Swanson, Henry Hanson, Martha Swanson, Butch ?, Carol ?, Jody ?, Steve Swanson, Esther Hanson, Margaret Swanson, Mrs. Burton and Henrietta Swanson. The Hanson home was a Quonset hut. *(Submitted by Chugiak-Eagle River Historical Society)*

(LEFT) Shot gun wedding: Harry (Bud) O'Donnell rides shotgun for his sister, Elizabeth, on her wedding day. She is marrying James H. Thornlow on July 4, 1948, in Palmer. With them is Elizabeth's mother, Valeria Ratliff (later Ulrich). Groom James was from Brooklyn, NY. He came to Alaska with Army-Air Force Rescue. Bride Elizabeth Ratliff came to Alaska in 1946 from Rhinelander, WI, accompanying her mother and several members of the family up the Alaska Highway. The wedding couple had three children who still live in Alaska: Chris Thornlow, Debbie Hobbs and Kathy Thornlow. (*Submitted by Kathy Thornlow*)

(ABOVE) Good-bye, Good-bye: In a scene that was repeated thousands of times, family and friends say farewell to passengers aboard the S.S. Yukon at the Seattle dock. The photo was taken from the deck of the Yukon on April 8, 1941. Many Alaskans would meet old friends on the vessel and the voyage would be something of a reunion. For those who had never been to Alaska, this scene could bring on anxiety - the realization that in moments their decision to head north would be irreversible. Editor Michael Carey's father, Fabian, came to Alaska for the first time on the Yukon in June 1937. (*Submitted by Chugiak-Eagle River Historical Society*)

(RIGHT) ENJOYING THE SLOPES: Mary Ann Michalek and Byron "Barney" Anderson pause during a ski excursion at Hatcher Pass near the Independence Mine. The year is 1946 or 1947. Barney worked at the mine, ran a shift at the powerhouse. The two married May 22, 1948, four days after Mary Ann graduated from high school. Barney's father was an original Matanuska Valley "colonist." The Andersons lived in Palmer all their lives. *(Submitted by Mary Ann Anderson)*

(ABOVE) A BOY IN OLD ANCHORAGE: Handsome Harold "Buzz" Jensen stands with his dog "Blackie" at 13th and H Street, Anchorage, in 1945. The houses behind him are still standing, although the view is different because of the growth of trees and foliage. "Buzz," born in Tanana, was the son of Pete and Sophia Jensen. He worked in Jim Moore's muffler shop for 30 years and was well known through his work. *(Submitted by Ilene Stackhouse)*

(LEFT) WEDDING BELLS: In the early 1940s, Elsie DeRoux Waldal (eldest daughter of Klondike miner August DeRoux) left Juneau for Anchorage to become a partner in the American Cleaners and Laundry at 234 Fourth Avenue. In 1942, she married Frank Brown, shown with her in this wedding photo. Frank later became one of Palmer's first city councilmen. Elsie, meanwhile, bought out her partners and re-named the business "Brown's Shop Furrier and Cleaners." *(Submitted by Joann Utt)*

(ABOVE) CAMPING ALONG THE ROAD: It's 1946, and here's one of the first families to drive the Alaska Highway from "the states" to Alaska. They are camping with a tarp spread out in lean-to fashion in case the weather turns foul. Pictured are Valeria Ratliff (later Ulrich), Adbelbert Ring and little Mary Ratliff. Adelbert had just been discharged from the Navy. *(Submitted by Kathy Thornlow)*

(RIGHT) FRIENDS AND CO-WORKERS: Ruth Westergaard, left, and Betty Semple were waitresses at the Star Cafe, a busy eatery located between B and C Streets on Fourth Avenue. In about 1948, probably on a holiday, they were photographed with Betty's son, John Phelps. Betty was from Fort Yukon. She had 10 children; eight live in the state, including John. Betty's children, youngest to oldest, are Sophie, Michael, Elisa, Audrey, Elva Fay, Joleen, Robbie, Marilyn, Donica and John. The Star Cafe, like so many other downtown Anchorage businesses, was a victim of the 1964 earthquake. Betty died in Seward in 1977. *(Submitted by John Phelps)*

(ABOVE) THE WHOLE STAFF WAS HERE: It was a pretty remarkable newspaper, The Adakian, the World War II military newspaper for American troops on the Aleutian Islands, soldiers at the end of the world. Seated, left to right: Bernard Kalb, Dashiell Hammett, Hal Sykes. Standing Alba Morris, Bill Glackens, Bernard Anastasia, Al Loefler, Jack (?), Oliver Pettigo, Don Miller. Miller was the cartoonist. Hammett was author of "The Maltese Falcon" and other classics, several of which were converted into major films. He was often called a radical, a communist - but he served his country well. Bernard Kalb had a long career in television journalist and as an best known for covering foreign affairs. Adak may have been a backwater, but it was important in all these men's lives. *(Submitted by the Blacks In Alaska History Project, George T. Harper, with permission)*

(LEFT) WORKING ON THE RAILROAD: Newly-married Helen Tollefsen stands near an Alaska Railroad sign announcing the section house at Kern, just south of Girdwood. It's the summer of 1948. Helen and her husband, Lester, were working for the railroad. Twenty-one-year-old Helen was a cook. She made about $2.20 an hour. He made about $2.30. The couple and their family lived in Talkeetna for many years. *(Submitted by Selinda Grenn)*

(ABOVE) MARKING A MEMORABLE DAY: Gov. Ernest Gruening signs the territory of Alaska's anti-discrimination bill in February 1945. Joining him are Elizabeth Peratrovich, Edward Anderson, Norman Walker and Roy Peratrovich. Elizabeth and husband Roy were instrumental in passage of the bill. Both had distinguished careers in public service. Among other things, Roy Peratrovich was first vice president of the Alaska Constitutional Convention. Anderson and Walker were on hand on behalf of the territorial House of Representatives and Senate. *(Submitted by Henry Kaiser Jr.)*

(ABOVE) WEDDING BELLS IN NINILCHIK: Nick Leman and Marian Broady are married Aug. 15, 1947. Marian's attendant is her twin sister, Margaret Broady (Lee). The twins came to Alaska in June 1946 as missionaries. Nick's attendant is his brother, Joe. Nick and Marian are the parents of Alaska's lieutenant governor, Loren Leman. *(Submitted by Loren Leman)*

(LEFT) THE WEAVERS HANDIWORK: Zelda Eidem, left, and Hilda Savela pose with their work, some time around 1948-1950. The scene is probably the Tanana Valley Fair in Fairbanks (which dates back to 1924). Zelda Eidem arrived in Golden Heart City in 1944. She helped establish the Presbyterian Church in College and the College Women's Club. Zelda moved to Pine Island, Minn., in 1965. Hilda Savela and her husband, John, also were long-time Fairbanks residents. *(Submitted by Greta Eidem)*

(RIGHT) HEADING FOR SEATTLE: A Mt. McKinley Airways DC-3 awaits passengers at Merrill Field in the 1940s. Pilot Pat Baker (uniform) and owner Jack Scavenius greet the passengers at the head of the stairs. Mt. McKinley flew from Anchorage to Seattle - with stops in Cordova and other cities - until competitors forced the company into bankruptcy. Owner Scavenius eventually became a lawyer. Note airline security in the era when Harry Truman was president - nonexistent. In some ways, the "old days" were not only simpler but better. *(Submitted by Peggy Burgin)*

(RIGHT) HE SERVED HIS COUNTRY: Charles T. Coleman stands on parade with fellow soldiers, probably during World War II. Born in Philadelphia, he served with Company A, 95th Engineer Regiment (GS colored), which helped build the Alaska Highway from the "states" to Alaska through Canada. He also served in the Pacific, winning three Bronze Stars. George Harper says, "Mr. Coleman was the only known black ALCAN veteran to return to Alaska to live." He lived in Anchorage and died there May 12, 2000. *(Submitted by the Blacks In Alaska History Project, George T. Harper, with permission)*

(ABOVE) HER FIRST STUDENTS: Lynn Locke (Meyer) took this photo of her fourth grade students in Hoonah during the 1949-1950 school year. Lynn came to Alaska from Vermont in 1949, so these were her first Alaska students. She married Gordon W. Meyer in 1951 and moved to Douglas. Lynn taught in Juneau schools until her retirement in 1977, more than a quarter century after meeting her first students. *(Submitted by Larry Meyer)*

(ABOVE) THE COOK WAS HERE: Johnny Jenkins, third from left second row, and some of his fellow sailors apparently were celebrating Christmas when this photo was taken. Jenkins, a sailor, rotated in and out of the Aleutian Islands from 1938 until 1944. He was a cook. Jenkins was on hand when the Japanese bombed Dutch Harbor. The fighting was fierce. Forty-three Americans were killed. Jenkins spent 24 years in the Navy, serving proudly. And he was proud of his cooking. "You couldn't win the war without the cook," he said. *(Submitted by the Blacks In Alaska History Project, George T. Harper, with permission)*

(RIGHT) A SUNNY DAY IN METLAKATLA: Maggie and George Williams enjoy a bit of warm weather in Metlakatla, sometime in the 1940s. The couple had a lengthy marriage. So did their son, Frank, who married Emma Kininnook, a student at the Chimawa school for Native Americans in Oregon. Frank and Emma were married 67 years, according to their granddaughter Harriett Fenerty of Anchorage (Maggie and George's great-granddaughter). *(Submitted by Harriett Fenerty)*

(ABOVE) THE KIDS ARE HERE: Three young travelers are about to get off an Alaska Airlines flight in Kodiak. It's Sept. 17, 1948. The kids are Carolyn Glover (Bernard), Pauline Glover (Penland), and Fred Glover Jr. They had flown to California to visit their grandparents. A postal official who met the kids wrote their parents, "I have never seen nicer behaved children than yours, and they were a joy to be around." *(Submitted by Carolyn Bernard)*

(ABOVE) JUST A FRIENDLY LITTLE GAME: Construction workers at the Kodiak naval base gather for their weekly poker game. The year was 1949. The Cold War sparked a military building boom that brought thousands of construction workers to Alaska. Employers often frowned on gambling - workers who lose their check are not happy workers - but the boss's disapproval did not stop men from playing cards. *(Submitted by John K. Marshall)*

(ABOVE) AN OUTING ON THE WATER: The kids are having fun on the north side of Lake Spenard, Anchorage. This was before there was a local pool, circa 1948. The kids - including Bonnie Tisler who still lives in Anchorage - were from the neighborhood. Editor Michael Carey, who grew up in Fairbanks, remembers playing in boats along the Chena River as a boy. Adults were horrified. They seemed to have one reaction: The kids are going to drown! *(Submitted by Bonnie Tisler)*

Submitted by Ruth Carson

THIS IS, TO CERTIFY THAT

PEGGY TURNER

IS A MEMBER IN GOOD STANDING

Inter-Airline Solidarity
Association
ANCHORAGE, ALASKA

1958

Submitted by Peggy Turner

WELLS FARGO
MESSENGER

MAY 1913

Submitted by Wells Fargo

ALASKA
STEAMSHIP COMPANY

Name

S.S. ALASKA   38

Sailing

Room

THE ALASKA LINE
SEATTLE

Submitted by John Jensen

The 1950's

Submitted by Philippa Wittmer Paige

(LEFT) READ ALL ABOUT IT: Young Caroleen Waterfield joins the ranks of "newsboys" outside the old federal building in Anchorage about 1952. The federal building contained the post office, where a long line of people gathered to get their mail. The people in line made ready customers for Caroleen. Some rough bars were nearby, which probably discouraged mothers from allowing their daughters to sell papers. But Caroleen's mother was nearby too - and she kept an eye on her daughter. *(Submitted by Caroleen Waterfield)*

(ABOVE) IN THE SWIM OF THINGS: Kids from the Palmer area celebrate a warm summer day in 1950. Pioneer Peak is in the background. In those days, Alaska had few government-built swimming pools. If you wanted to swim, the best place was a gravel pit, like this one. Typically, gravel-pit water was clean and safe enough - but oh did it get cold near the bottom of the pit. Bob Wimmer is the boy facing the camera. Bob now lives in Oregon. *(Submitted by Robert and Joan Wimmer)*

(RIGHT) STARS OF THE DIMOND: Rick (left) and Mick Petitt assume a professional pose with Lazy Mountain in the background, near Palmer. Rick played for Koslosky's store, Mick for the Kiwanis team. Both boys later excelled in high school sports. An Anchorage Times clipping says that as a basketball player, Mick once scored 30 points against Wasilla. Rick later became a "baseball diplomat," coaching briefly in Nicaragua and taking a team to Japan. His artistic skills also were such that in 1968 he was a guest artist at Anchorage's Paintin' Place Gallery. *(Submitted by Jack Seemann)*

(LEFT) PORTRAIT OF A MERCHANT: Leon Urbach had a lot to do with making Alaska. Born in Nebraska in 1885, he came to Alaska in 1915 and opened a successful store in Seward. He was president of the Seward Chamber of Commerce and chairman of the local Selective Service Board. A Republican, he nevertheless made his home a meeting place for people of all political persuasions. The Anchorage Times said that when Seward didn't have a newspaper, "it was Leon who got up early each morning, gleaned the national news from his radio, and posted it on his window for all to share." A most conscientious thing to do. But then over the decades, the Urbach family was conscientiously involved in public affairs. *(Submitted by Dorothy Urbach)*

(LEFT) THE PROUD GRADUATES: Graduates of Seward High School, Margaret Lindsey (now Anderson) and Bill Erwin hold their diplomas. Margaret remained in Seward where she and her husband were active in fishing and fish processing. She also served on the city council. Bill went off to the big city - Anchorage - where he became a lawyer. He still lives in Anchorage. Margaret and Bill not only graduated together. They were born the same day in 1933 and attended 12 years of school together. *(Submitted by Margaret Lindsey Anderson)*

(ABOVE) A FAMILY PORTRAIT: The Piaskowski family stands for a family photo at their homestead on the Old Seward Highway in 1958. Bob and Shirley Piaskowski had 11 children. Most of the children still live in Alaska. Bob and Shirley also have 27 grandchildren and 7 great-grandchildren. Bob retired from civil service on Elmendorf Air Force Base. He was in maintenance for the Air Force. *(Submitted by Shirley L. Piaskowski)*

(RIGHT) **THEY CALLED IT HOME:** Mary Huddleston stands in front of a 16-by-16 foot tent that she and her family lived in for three years. The location is near Copper Center, the year 1952. Mary cooked on a Coleman stove, the family hauled water. One winter, the temperature dropped to -72 degrees. Mary's daughter Joan says, "The life we left in Minnesota and what we had in Alaska were extremely different but we were the better for it and never looked back." *(Submitted by Joan M. Schilling)*

(ABOVE) **THE WATERMAN AT WORK:** A man identified only as "David" gets water for the community, either Beaver or Fort Yukon. The picture was taken in the 1950s. Yukon River water tastes pretty good when it has had a chance to settle. Note the use of 5-gallon gasoline cans. Today, that practice no doubt would make health officials unhappy but was standard back then - as was the practice of collecting rainwater in 55-gallon drums. *(Submitted by Charlie Mayse Collection)*

(LEFT) OUT FOR A DRIVE: Elva Titus, a Fairbanks lawyer, stands next to a car associated with one of the great symbols of '50s Alaska, the DEWLINE or Distant Early Warning Line. The DEWLINE was constructed to warn the United States of a Soviet attack on the United States. DEWLINE sites were all over Alaska. Federal Electric was a major DEWLINE contractor. The photo was taken near Fairbanks. Elva was a Fairbanks lawyer who worked for the colorful lawyer and legislator Warren Taylor. Sadly, she died young. *(Submitted by Ben and Kay Rosey)*

(RIGHT) THE BRASS CHAT: Maj. Gen. William Kepner, left, confers with Col. Lars L. Johnson, commander of the Alaska National Guard, in Johnson's Juneau office, 1952. Kepner was commander-in-chief of the Alaska Command, assuming that position June 1, 1950. During his lengthy military career, the Indiana native witnessed the complete transformation of war. The horse was still crucial to warfare when he served on the Mexican border during World War I. In 1946, Kepner was in charge of air operations for the atomic bomb tests at Bikini in the South Pacific. Johnson, a World War II combat pilot, was appointed the guard's adjutant general in 1951. He had a long career in both military and civilian aviation in Alaska, working for the FAA and Alaska Airlines. He eventually became state director of aviation during the administration of Gov. Bill Egan. *(Submitted by Gordon D. Homme)*

(RIGHT) THE OFFICE STAFF: Northwest Airlines employees gather in the office at the old Westward Hotel, now the Anchorage Hilton. Elmer Sellin, freight manager, and "Cot" Hayes, Alaska sales manager, are standing. Lloyd Smith, Anchorage sales manager, and secretary Betty Kampfer are sitting. Anchorage was just evolving as an international aviation hub when this photo was taken in 1953. Back then, Northwest crew members had long layovers in Anchorage - sometimes four days. Elmer Sellin was with Northwest's Anchorage staff from 1950-1962. He was a member of the School Board, president of the Anchorage High School PTA, and co-founder of Anchorage Toastmasters. *(Submitted by Peg Turner)*

(LEFT) EASTER EGGS ON ICE: Children in the village of Solomon, near Nome, gather for a group photo after an Easter-egg hunt in 1951 or 1952. Judging from their faces, these kids were having fun. Frank Walker, the local Bureau of Indian Affairs teacher, took the photo. Frank and his wife, Lillian, taught in many rural communities including Solomon and Kalskag on the Kuskokwim River. *(Submitted by Bruce Walker)*

(LEFT) AT YOUR SERVICE: Bill Mueller stands in front of his cab, somewhere in Anchorage. Perhaps at the dispatch office located at Fourth Avenue and C Street. Canteen Cab was an early taxi company. The percentage of residents who owned a car - let alone two cars - was smaller in those days, so the taxi played an important role in local transportation. Note the simple telephone number: Main 699. *(Submitted by Judy Jett)*

(ABOVE) JUNIOR LAWMAN: Bob Nesvick enjoys the view along Fourth Avenue in Anchorage in 1954, Fur Rendezvous time. Bob was an Alaska state trooper from 1974 until 1990, serving in Anchorage, Fairbanks, Palmer, Haines, Juneau, Ketchikan and Glennallen. From 1993 until 1995, he was the police chief in Metlakatla. He now serves in federal law enforcement. *(Submitted by Robert Nesvick)*

(ABOVE) FROM THE DUGOUT TO THE FIELD: The 1954 Little League State Champions head for the field for the first game of the Alaska Little League Baseball tournament. Left to right Wayne Lewis, Donny Ryan, Dave Shackleton, J.C. Bell, Tom Gebhart, Mike Shupe and Donnie Cartee. The club, managed by Pat Cartee and coached by Dick Bacon, won the territorial tournament and represented Alaska in the regional tournament in Vancouver, British Columbia. Lewis, Bell, Shupe and Cartee all live in Anchorage. *(Submitted by Dan Cartee)*

(LEFT) A SUMMER OUTING: The Phillips and Lonas families were neighbors in Mountain View who shared similar interests. Newcomers to Alaska, they enjoyed camping in summer, card games in winter. Here they are visiting Eklutna Lake: Individually, they are Bud Phillips holding Johnna Lonas, Alice Phillips holding Nicki, and Jeanie Phillips and Charlene Lonas holding Mary Lonas. The Phillipses were from California, and eventually went back. The photo was taken about 1952. *(Submitted by Herbert Atchison)*

(RIGHT) GIVE 'EM A LEFT, GIVE 'EM A RIGHT: Junior pugilists are at it in front of a big crowd in Bethel one Fourth of July in the 1950s. Boxing was one of the many activities that day. This is another vivid example of just how homemade entertainment was before statehood. It would be delightful if somebody could tell us who some of these folks are - and what became of them. *(Submitted by Pioneer Memorial Park Inc. Batchelder Collection)*

BELOW) **SMILE FOR THE CAMERA:** Mary Lonas
tands by the family DeSoto in about 1953. Her father, John,
ook the picture. John was from Tennessee and lives there now.
With his wife, Charlene, he settled in Mountain View after
oming to Anchorage. He worked for an Anchorage painting
ompany for a number of years. Mary still lives in Anchorage.
(Submitted by Herbert Atchison)

(ABOVE) **A COMMUNITY POTLUCK ON THE FOURTH:** The Bethel
Chamber of Commerce and friends put on a community celebration of
Independence Day sometime in the 1950s. Bethel sits on the Kuskokwim River.
Moravian missionaries who arrived in the 1880s bestowed the name Bethel on the
town. In 1950, Bethel had a population of 651. Looks like just about everybody was
there on this Fourth of July. *(Submitted by Pioneer Memorial Park Inc. Batchelder Collection)*

(LEFT) **TAKING AIM:** Outdoorsman and writer Charlie Mayse (1906-1990) photographed this boy at Kaktovik on the Beaufort Sea in the early to mid 1950s. Mayse trapped for more than 30 years in and around Beaver. He traveled all over Alaska. His writing, based on his experience, frequently appeared in Alaska Magazine. He also took hundreds of photographs, many of Native children at play or mugging for the camera. It is unfortunate that Charlie did not record the name of this little guy. Wouldn't you like to know? *(Submitted by Charlie Mayse Collection)*

(RIGHT) **A HOT DAY ON THE JOB:** These unidentified men were hard at work on a hot day in Bethel back in the mid-'50s. They were working on the school. Perhaps the two were typical of the '50s construction workers - men who made good wages in summer, then lived on "rockin' chair money" (unemployment checks) in winter. T. S. Batchelder, a contractor who worked all over Alaska, took the photo. Batchelder took his camera wherever he went. *(Submitted by Pioneer Memorial Park Inc. Batchelder Collection)*

(BELOW) PAVING THE WAY TO PROGRESS: Rudy Mallonee (foreground) and unknown co-workers are hard at it on the job. The men were paving a section of the Richardson Highway between Copper Center and Gulkana in 1951. Rudy was a mechanic and welder. He and his family lived in a trailer during construction and moved as the job progressed. During the '50s, opportunities for construction workers abounded because of the many military projects - and because of projects like this one. *(Submitted by Duffie Mallonee)*

(ABOVE) HERE COMES THE BUS: In the late '50s, Robert and Edna Williams ran the first school bus in Anchor Point. Mrs. Williams was the driver. The couple also owned a hardware store. The bus picked up students along the Sterling Highway and North Fork Road. The scene is a good depiction of just how rural the Kenai Peninsula was in the '50s. *(Submitted by Carol Schmidt)*

(LEFT) HEADED UP IN THE AIR: Mac McIver and five of his seven daughters await a flight at the Nome airport, 1952. Wallace McIver handled building mechanics at the Nome hospital for many years and mined. The girls are, clockwise, Gail, Kay, Janice, Barbie and baby Cheryl in daddy's arms. The girls' grandparents were well-known missionaries, L.E. Ost and his wife Ruth. *(Submitted by Elin Headrick)*

(ABOVE) ENJOYING THE HOLIDAY: Residents of Bethel take in the Fourth of July in the 1950s. Their attire suggests this Fourth was chilly if not outright cold. In her book "Bethel: The First Hundred Years," Mary Lenz quotes Jimmy Pete as saying, "Fourth of July we used to go to Napakiak because they had their Fourth of July on the Third. The Bethel Fourth would be on the Fourth. That way everybody could go down and celebrate Napakiak's Fourth of July and then next day come up to celebrate Bethel's." *(Submitted by Pioneer Memorial Park Inc. Batchelder Collection)*

(RIGHT) MODELING NEW OUTFITS: Brothers "Bing" and Esias Henry of Beaver were all smiles in their new outfits when this photo was taken in Beaver, about 1953. Trapper, outdoorsman and writer Charlie Mayse, who lived in Beaver, was the photographer. Note the identical attire, which probably came by mail from Sears. Wonderful outfits, wonderful kids. *(Submitted by Charlie Mayse Collection)*

(ABOVE) A PARADE ON THE FOURTH: Independence Day always calls for a parade, and this parade was on July 4, 1951. The parade not only celebrated American independence from Britain but also honored the fight for Alaska statehood, which was not won until 1959. Here the Future Dairymen are aboard a float making its way through the streets. One wonders how many of the young people actually grew up to be dairymen. *(Submitted by Dottie Hill)*

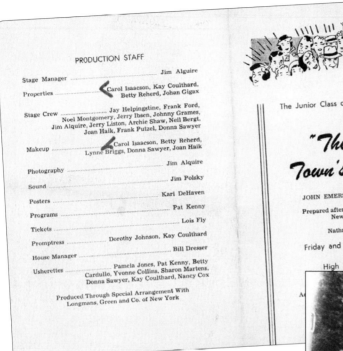

PRODUCTION STAFF

Stage Manager .... Jim Alguire

Properties .... Carol Isaacson, Kay Coulthard, Betty Reherd, Johan Gigax

Stage Crew .... Jay Helpingstine, Frank Ford, Noel Montgomery, Jerry Ibsen, Johnny Grames, Jim Alguire, Jerry Liston, Archie Shaw, Nell Bergt, Joan Haik, Frank Putzel, Donna Sawyer

Makeup .... Carol Isaacson, Betty Reherd, Lynne Briggs, Donna Sawyer, Joan Haik

Photography .... Jim Alguire

Sound .... Jim Polsky

Posters .... Karl DeHaven

Programs .... Pat Kenny

Tickets .... Lois Fly

Promptress .... Dorothy Johnson, Kay Coulthard

House Manager .... Bill Dresser

Usherettes .... Pamela Jones, Pat Kenny, Betty Cardullo, Yvonne Collins, Sharon Martens, Donna Sawyer, Kay Coulthard, Nancy Cox

Produced Through Special Arrangement With Longmans, Green and Co. of New York

The Junior Class of Anchorage High School

presents

"The Whole Town's Talking"

by

JOHN EMERSON AND ANITA LOOS

Prepared after the manner of the original New York production
by
Nathaniel Edward Reeid

Friday and Saturday, March 20-21
8:00 P.M.
High School Auditorium

(LEFT) THE JUNIOR CLASS PLAY: Anchorage High School - when there was one high school - put on John Emerson and Anita Loos' "The Whole Town is Talking" for family, friends and just about anyone who wanted to see theater. The play's co-author, Anita Loos (1893-1981), deserves special mention. She is known for "Gentlemen Prefer Blondes," which made the phrase a permanent part of the English language. Her autobiography , "A Girl Like I," is written with the humor and self-mockery the title implies. *(Submitted by Caroleen Waterfield)*

(RIGHT) A MEMENTO OF HER FIRST VISIT: The Williams' children stand with their grandmother, Molly Canon, during her first visit to Alaska in 1957. The scene is the gas station in Anchor Point. From left to right: Bonnie Williams, Molly Canon, Gary Williams and Carol Williams. Robert and Edna Williams were the children's parents. Edna took the photograph. *(Submitted by Carol Schmidt)*

(RIGHT) THE MADHATTER'S PARTY: This is the Girl Scouts mad hatter party, circa 1954. The location is seventh and Barrow, Anchorage. Bonnie Weimer (now Tisler) is third from the left in the front row. From left to right front row: Patricia Cavanaugh, Judy Grisham, Bonnie Weimer, Elaine Atwood and Gladys Kavara. Back row: unknown, Sonja Hopkins, June Boudish - and the rest are unknown. Bonnie Weimer came from a pioneering family. She still lives in Anchorage. *(Submitted by Bonnie Tisler)*

(LEFT) GIRLS OF GOODNEWS BAY: Trapper, outdoorsman, and writer Charlie Mayse took this photo on one of his many trips around the Last Frontier. The time is probably the mid-'50s. During his almost 50 years in Alaska, Mayse canoed the Yukon River from the headwaters to the mouth. The girls are unnamed. Perhaps that won't be the case much longer - perhaps someone reading this book will recognize them. *(Submitted by Charlie Mayse Collection)*

(LEFT) MUSH, MUSH YOU HUSKIES: Mary Joyce drives her dogs in downtown Juneau as part of a 1959 statehood parade. Mary had an exceptional life. She came to Alaska in 1928 and became an accomplished musher and outdoorswoman as well as a stewardess for Northwest Airlines. In 1936-'37, she mushed a 5-dog team from Taku Lodge, near Juneau, to Fairbanks, more than 1,000 miles. Temperatures reached 50 below zero on the trail. When asked why she made the trip, she replied, "I just wanted to see if I could do it." She also mushed dogs in tamer locations - Sun Valley and St. Paul, Minn. Mary died in 1976. *(Submitted By Bruce Campbell)*

(RIGHT) ROGERS AND HAMMERSTEIN IN ALASKA: It's Sept. 15, 1951, at Elmendorf Air Force Base and this is the opening number of the second act of the great "South Pacific." The performers are servicemen from all branches of the military and their family members, with just two exceptions. Kodiak, Adak, Ladd Air Force Base (now Fort Wainwright) played host to "South Pacific" before the touring troop, organized by the 17th Naval District, appeared at Elmendorf. A newspaper story of the day described Ruth Wichelmann as the "singing star of the show." *(Submitted by Ruth Carson)*

(RIGHT) KEEPING IN STEP: The Shriners are looking good and working together on the Fourth of July 1951. This scene is truly downtown Anchorage. Note the old federal building in the distance. Today, new businesses prevail on this block, including Kumagoro, Stewart's Photo and the Downtown Deli. This part of town was re-arranged by, among other things, the 1964 Good Friday earthquake. *(Submitted by Josephine "Dean" Alsobrook)*

(LEFT) SCHOOL DAYS OF YESTERYEAR: Rudy Dean Mallonee (back row, center) and his sister Joan Mallonee (first row, right, in front of Rudy) are with classmates in front of the Copper Center territorial school in 1951. Rudy Dean went on to become a builder. In recent years, he has split time between Wasilla and Costa Rica. Joan married and left Alaska. She now lives in Greenville, Texas. The school may have been small but the kids' faces tell us hopes were high. *(Submitted by Duffie Mallonee)*

(LEFT) THE ARTIST AT HOME: Painter Fred Machetanz and his wife, Sara, pose with their dog, Seegoo, outside their home in Palmer during the summer of 1952. Fred and Sara were just finishing up construction. Emily Harvey took the photo. Emily and her brother Bob drove the Alaska Highway with their father in 1952. The Machetanzs, whom the family had heard lecture in Memphis, Tenn., had inspired them. Fred and Sara said, "Come see us if you ever are in Alaska." The Harveys did. Bob Harvey now lives in Anchorage. *(Submitted by Bob Harvey)*

(ABOVE) WORKING INTO THE WINTER: Dredge Number 6 at Ester, west of Fairbanks, worked into December 1956 and Robert Robb, now of Anchorage, was a crew member. The United States Smelting Refining and Mining Co., once a big player in the Alaska gold industry, operated the dredge. Visitors to the Ester area can still see the large cuts where mining occurred. Young Robb - he was 21 - drove a "cat" part of the time. The work took up lots of his time. Seven days a week, 12 hours a day, and the pay was all straight time, $1.76 an hour. *(Submitted by Robert T. Robb)*

(LEFT) SAYING HELLO TO THE NEIGHBORS: Emily Harvey poses between Jack Ross and his wife, Sylvia, in a Fairbanks trailer court, 1951. The Harveys and Rosses were neighbors. Jack Ross was promoting oil and gas development through the Fairbanks Oil and Gas Co. In cooperation with stateside investors, the Fairbanks group, including Ross, leased 250,000 acres of land for exploration in the Kateel River area west of Fairbanks. Optimism brimmed but the field never produced a barrel. Emily Harvey lived in Iowa, Texas, and Indiana before retiring to Florida. *(Submitted by Bob Harvey)*

(RIGHT) A BUSY MAN TAKES A BREAK: Rudy Mallonee stands next to a truck owned by J. H. Pomeroy in the summer of 1952. Rudy was working for Pomeroy on a military construction job in Kenai. He was a mechanic and welder - much appreciated for his skills. On this job, he ran the shop. Later he owned his own business in Anchorage, Rudy's Shop at 72nd and Arctic, where he made many friends. *(Submitted by Duffie Mallonee)*

(LEFT) THE KIDS OF DOWNTOWN PALMER: Mick, Rick and Collie Pettit peer intently into the camera from the back of a truck. The scene is downtown Palmer. Mick went on to become a teacher and coach. Rick worked for the state department of transportation. After retirement, he opened his own business. Collie Pettit (Johansen) married and lives in Anchorage. Jack Seemann, their stepfather, wrote on a note accompanying this photo: "My wonderful stepchildren." A lovely thought, a lovely picture. *(Submitted by Jack Seemann)*

(RIGHT) JUST TAKING A LITTLE BREAK: Employees of the H and D Market on I Street were always busy but had time for the camera on this day. Bob and Shirley Horrell, who went into business after World War II, owned the market. Bob was inspired to drive the Alaska Highway with a load of supplies - that's how the market started. At first, Bob and Shirley lived above the store. From left to right in the photograph: Bob Horrell, Trudy Fritz, Ray Leonard and Tex Bearden. *(Submitted by Joyce Horrell)*

(ABOVE) BACK ON THE BUS: Margaret "Peggy" Lynch and her daughter Kathleen are on their way back to the Matanuska Valley Bus Line coach after stopping at the Eureka Road House. They were travelling to Valdez from Anchorage, with husband and dad Ed. The Eureka Road House was at mile 81 of the Glenn Highway says Tewkesbury's 1948 directory of Alaska businesses. The Lynchs bused it to Valdez one day, came back the next. Ed represented Firestone Tire and Rubber for many years. Russ Swank owned the bus. *(Submitted by Ed Lynch)*

(BELOW) STRUTTIN' THIER STUFF: A rooster and a chicken are out in their finest at the state fair in Palmer. Whoops, this was 1951 when Alaska was a territory. There was a fair but no "state fair." To celebrate successful agriculture and animal husbandry, these two characters were made part of the show. *(Submitted by Wanda Anderson Wheeler)*

(ABOVE) BOB, THE BEAR, AND THE BLONDE: It's the old soft shoe for Bob Hope and Jayne Mansfield who find themselves, appropriately enough in Alaska, dancing with a "bear." The entertainers were putting on a show at Elmendorf Air Force Base in 1959 around Christmas. Hope performed at hundreds of these service shows during his long career. He was in Alaska a number of times going back to World War II. *(Submitted by Betty J. Combs)*

(ABOVE) THOSE WILD AND CRAZY REPUBLICAN WOMEN: The Republican Women's Club can see that President Eisenhower's chance of re-election is excellent. The occasion is a luncheon; the date, July 14, 1956. Alaskans, as residents of a territory, could not vote in the presidential election. They made their views known and raised money for the national parties nonetheless. The second woman from the right is Zelda Eidem (who, in keeping with the spirit of the times, is identified on the back of the photo by her husband's name - Mrs. Nick Eidem). Fairbanks banker Bill Stroecker remembers Zelda as "a civic dynamo." *(Submitted by Greta Eidem)*

(LEFT) A DEFINITE CONTRAST IN STYLES: A C-47 Air Force cargo plane and a local dog team stand in sharp contrast on St. Lawrence Island in 1955. The aircraft had just completed delivering supplies to airmen stationed at Northeast Cape. For many servicemen, scenes like this vividly illustrated just how different Alaska was from their home states. *(Submitted by Dale Hillmer)*

(RIGHT) GATHERED WITH PRIDE: Staff members at Carr's, 13th and Gambell, stand for a professional photographer, Ward Wells, on a nice day in about 1958. Larry Carr, whose name is synonymous with the Alaska grocery business, is at the far right end of the first row. Del Martinson, second from the left in the top row, was general manager. Del departed Carr's in 1965 to join his wife in her business, Alaska Party Sales, which sold the ever-popular, indispensable Tupperware. *(Submitted by Ruth and Del Martinson)*

(RIGHT) PILOTS AND DAUGHTER: Marjorie Ann Steinbrecher, her daughter, Janice, and husband, Robert, enjoy a lighter moment in the summer of 1951. Robert was a pilot for Reeve Aleutian Airways. Marjorie was a pilot, too. She trained at Merrill Field for a commercial license. After she qualified in 1950, the Anchorage Times wrote a story "Anchorage Mother Wins Commercial Pilot's License," noting she was the first woman in Alaska to receive the license. Marjorie was pregnant when she took the course and gave birth shortly following certification - to the astonishment of her flight instructor. Although qualified, she never did pilot commercial flights.

(Submitted by Jan O'Hara)

(BELOW) A CHRISTMAS OF YESTERYEAR: Jack and Sylvia Gwaltney of Anchorage pose next to their tree in the Christmas season of 1958. Jack was a leader in the insurance business. He and Sylvia still volunteer for many civic and social causes in Anchorage. Their son David and his sons, Sean and Brian, all live in Anchorage.

(Submitted by Tom Robbins)

(ABOVE) OFF WE GO, INTO THE WILD BLUE YONDER: The McKinley kids are flying in their airplane - their imaginary airplane, Kodiak 1953. Velda McKinley (Brown), is the left wing, Dale the pilot, Mike the engine and Danny the wing. The kids' father was the local deputy U.S. marshal. There are eight McKinley children, seven born in Kodiak. Four of the eight now live in Alaska. *(Submitted by Velda Brown)*

(BELOW) A FACE TO REMEMBER: Olga Nikolai Ezi, born in 1875, was from the Copper River Valley, near Tyone Lake. Wanda Anderson Wheeler, who was at that time a newcomer, took this photo in 1950. "Grandma Ezi," as she was known, was from a family that at one time migrated all the way to Cook Inlet to obtain a winter supply of fish, the last people known to do so. They had a fish camp at what is now Point Woronzof. Olga married Simeon Esi (later changed to Ezi). In later years, she lived with a granddaughter near Eklutna. Wanda Anderson Wheeler took this photo after she obtained Grandma Ezi's permission. Wanda still lives in Alaska. *(Submitted by Wanda Anderson Wheeler)*

(LEFT) A MINI FIESTA: Patrick and Leeann Belgard celebrate "Fiesta Day" at the playground, 10th Avenue and E Street, 1955. Anchorage was growing rapidly in the years right after the Korean War. Finding places for children to play safely was difficult, but community leaders did take time to provide playgrounds as Anchorage expanded. *(Submitted by Catherine Belgard)*

(RIGHT) KIDS AT HOME, AT PLAY:
The four De Vries children stand next to their Lazy Mountain home outside of Palmer. In back, David and Andrew, in front, Marie (now Keen) and John De Vries, Jr. Their father, John, was a vocational education teacher, their mother, Jessie, a nurse. Andrew now lives in Oregon; his sister and two brothers live in Alaska. *(Submitted by Jessie De Vries)*

(LEFT) POURING IT ON: Katy Harbeson pours the cement floor on the family home near Wasilla, 1959. Katy and her husband, George, came to Alaska from New Jersey in 1954. He was a teacher. The Harbesons became briefly disenchanted with Alaska and left. They returned, however, to settle for good, homesteading and building this house. For the Harbesons, the place was home for 30 years. Their five children - George Jr., LeeAnna, Richard, Rebecca and Peter - all live in Alaska. *(Submitted by Rebecca Chapman)*

(RIGHT) GETTING AFTER THE GOLD: Jim Hansen is busy working at the family mine on Crooked Creek of the Seventymile River. The river was so named by miners because the mouth is 70 miles down the Yukon River from Fort Reliance, Canada. Young Jim completed high school in Fairbanks and went on to become a commercial pilot, flying for Wien Airlines among others. He maintained his interest in mining, however, and worked ground on the Seward Peninsula. Today, Jim lives in Nome. *(Submitted by Jim Hansen)*

(RIGHT) TAKING A LITTLE BREAK: Airman Dale Hillmer takes a break from unloading a military cargo plane that had landed at Northeast Cape on St. Lawrence Island. Hillmer, a South Dakota boy, was stationed on the island in 1954-1955. He was a radio intercept operator, but anyone off duty was expected to unload supplies. *(Submitted by Dale Hillmer)*

(ABOVE) KINDERGARTEN KIDS: It's time for the annual May Poll dance in Fairbanks and kindergarteners were well-attired in the early '50s. The scene was right outside the old Main School, which is now the Fairbanks City Hall. Wilma Thompson, who taught the class, was in Fairbanks until 1954 when she and her husband moved to the Kenai Peninsula to homestead. She taught in Kenai until retirement at age 65 then opened a private kindergarten. *(Submitted by Greta Eidem)*

(RIGHT) A MOMENT WITH THE CHAMP: John Marshall, left, and his son Gary are joined by heavyweight champion Jack Dempsey at Dempsey's Restaurant in New York, 1955. John Marshall was in the Navy, stationed on Kodiak. He and his son were vacationing. Dempsey's restaurant in midtown Manhattan drew people from all over the world to see the living legend who owned it. On at least one occasion, a mugger who thought he saw a vulnerable old man wound up eating his own teeth. John Marshall spent many years with the Navy and is now retired in Anchorage.

(Submitted by John K. Marshall)

(LEFT) GET YOUR FRESH WATER: Lester Bronson delivers fresh, clean water to the people of Nome in the 1950s. Many Alaska cities had poor water in the '50s. Well water was often full of minerals that affected taste and appearance. If you needed water in Nome you called MAIN 19 - or put a card with a "W" in the window. Bronson was sure to come and deliver the "W." *(Submitted by Kathleen Hansen)*

(LEFT) COUPLE OF KIDS ON A NICE DAY: Sandra Wheeler (now Quimby) and Vikki Hosman (now Solberg) stand proudly together in July 1958. Sandra's mother, Wanda Anderson Wheeler, took the photo. Sandra lives in Eagle River; she is the mother of four children. Vikki, who lives in Anchorage, has 11 children. She also is the owner of The Natural Pantry in Anchorage. *(Submitted by Wanda Anderson Wheeler)*

(BELOW RIGHT) GET OUT AND VOTE: Stickers that say "I voted" are common on Election Day. But this one is unique. It was a piece of the first Alaska state election in 1958, just after Alaskans approved statehood. Only 50,000 voters participated but they were courted by the likes of John Kennedy and Richard Nixon. Nixon even drove a dog team as part of the Republican effort to drum up support. For the GOP, the results were miserable. The day after the election the Fairbanks Daily News-Miner, a partisan Republican paper, said "Voters Speak Democratic." Democrats carried every statewide office and 52 of the 60 legislative seats. The legendary Bill Egan won the first of his three terms as governor. *(Submitted by John T. Jensen)*

Submitted by Gale K. Vick

1960's-1970's

Submitted by Tam Agosti-Gisler

Submitted by Wanda Anderson Wheeler

(LEFT) A MOMENT OF RECOGNITION: James E. Malone receives an award from the Incentive Awards Committee at Ft. Richardson, 1962. Presenting the award is Kenneth McGuire. Malone, who worked at the power plant, had ideas about how to improve safely, cleanliness, and employee morale. Malone's suggestions dealt with how the coal should be handled, particularly because the old system wasted time, spread coal dust and was dangerous. (*Submitted by the Blacks In Alaska History Project, George T. Harper, with permission*)

(RIGHT) GET YOUR MOTOR RUNNIN': Golden Hudson has his motor running aboard a Honda Trail 90 motorcycle. The pack on his back shows he has been a successful caribou hunter. The date was 1966, the photographer hunting partner Milt Stevens. The two men hunted for years off the Denali Highway, covering vast amounts of territory on their cycles. This was before the 3-wheeler or the 4-wheeler was available. The caribou was taken 20 miles from the highway: a serious hike if you didn't have a motorcycle. (*Submitted by Beverly Stevens*)

(RIGHT) FOLLOWING THE TRADITIONAL MODEL: Unnamed fishermen from the village of Kasigluk, west of Bethel, dip for dinner in 1964. The day looks chilly - but the men kept at their task. Note the dog sitting in the background. The dog would not cross windblown, snowless ice while part of a dog team, so he was staked on the ice until he became accustomed to the smooth surface. *(Submitted by Bruce Walker)*

(LEFT) MISS ALASKA HAS ARRIVED: Collie Pettit (Johansen), Miss Alaska, greets President Lyndon Johnson, Washington 1967. Alaska congressman Howard Pollock is to the left. Behind Pollock is Lorene Harrison, Collie's chaperone. Sen. Bob Bartlett is in the background, mostly obscured. In the course of traveling, Collie and Lorene became very good friends. Collie grew up in the Matanuska Valley and now lives in Anchorage. She maintains an interest in gardening from her "valley" days. *(Submitted by Jack Seemann)*

(LEFT) A CELEBRITY MOOSE: Dr. Judith Samter and Mother Moose sat down together for a brief chat. Mother Moose was a popular television character in Anchorage years ago. She made frequent public appearances. Samter has a doctorate in special education. She taught in that field for almost 30 years. *(Submitted by Dr. Judith E. Samter)*

(ABOVE) FINDING A WAY TO WIN: The famed World Eskimo Indian Olympics were in their infancy when this photograph was taken in 1964. Unfortunately, the names of the competitors are not known. The Olympics have become very popular with Alaskans and visitors. They are not only entertaining but educational, providing a window on traditional cultures. *(Submitted by Bruce Walker)*

(RIGHT) KEEPING AN EYE OUT: A young soldier from Fort Richardson polices downtown Anchorage after the March 1964 earthquake. In the background is the Anchorage Westward Hotel, now the Anchorage Hilton. The earthquake stunned thousands of people and created chaos. The military was called in to provide discipline and protection. It's fair to say that the D&D Bar behind the soldier no longer offered a cafe or TV. It wasn't D&D - it was D-E-A-D. *(Submitted by the Blacks In Alaska History Project, George T. Harper, with permission)*

(LEFT) IT WAS ANOTHER ERA: In 1960, the legislative wives - and the women legislators - posed for a group photo in Juneau. The governor and lieutenant governor's wives were there, too. Legislators are Irene Ryan, fourth from left back row, Blanche McSmith, eighth from left back row, and Helen Fischer, fifth from left front row. Madge Wade and Neva Egan, wives to the lieutenant governor and governor are in the front row, third and fourth from the left. Legislative wives include Arne Beltz (first row far left) and Bella Hammond and Carolyn Rader (end of the last row). *(Submitted by LaRue Hellenthal)*

(RIGHT) DRESSED FOR THE OCCASION: It's opening night at the Lampost Inn Restaurant at mile 14.5 on the Glenn Highway, 1961. Walter Bowen built the place, starting in 1959. The waitress on the right was the chef's wife, but does anyone know the women's names? Marion Bowen made the waitresses' dresses. Marion remembers, "The carpet was a brown and beige blend commercial type. Most of the local people who came were hesitant to come in on the carpet as it was unusual to have in a restaurant at the time." (*Submitted by Marion Bowen*)

(ABOVE) THE GIANT HAS LANDED: Aviation was crucial to North Slope oil development. Here an Alaska Airlines cargo flight is unloading as oil exploration proceeds. Flights from Fairbanks brought in men, materials and equipment, especially in the days before completion of the Dalton Highway to the North Slope. Note the isolation of the scene. No wonder some of those who worked on the North Slope in the early stages of development thought they had come to the end of the earth. (*Submitted by Gil Mull*)

(LEFT) HANDING OUT AN AWARD: Fairbanks radio personality Bill Walley and the national president of the National Defense Transportation Association, Ken Vore, exchange handshakes as Sen. Bob Bartlett (left) looks on. The association promoted transportation for defense purposes and civil defense. This photo was taken at the annual convention in Fairbanks in 1967. Walley went on to a long career in broadcasting and became mayor of Fairbanks. *(Submitted by Ben and Kay Rosey)*

(RIGHT) METER MAIDS PREPARE FOR ACTION: Anchorage's first meter maids are reading for work, 1961. They are Audrey Jones, Francis Macon and Trudy Wolfe. The meter maids were part of the modernization of Anchorage after statehood in 1959, although the folks who received tickets no doubt didn't think so. Over the years, the meter maids proved both efficient and necessary. Some drivers always will overstay their welcome if the government doesn't give them an "incentive" to move. *(Submitted by Judy Jett)*

(RIGHT) TAKING IN THE HARVEST:
Dave Pippel stacks oats on the Pippel family farm, Eagle River, 1963. Walter Pippel started clearing land in this area in 1945. The farm is now all gone to commercial development. And to think that Dave Pippel once had an 1,800-foot airstrip on the farm, a strip on which he learned to fly. *(Submitted by Dave Pippel)*

(LEFT) WAKE UP AND SMELL THE COFFEE: Members of the wake-up crew at the National Defense Transportation Association convention are ready to serve. The date is 1967 in Fairbanks. Left to right: Leona Chapados, Connie Kopf, Mel Harris, and Virginia Harris. The association promoted defense transportation, a crucial matter to Alaska then and now. *(Submitted by Ben and Kay Rosey)*

(RIGHT) HIS FIRST TRIP: John L. Harris of California made his first visit to Alaska in the early 1960s to visit his family. With him is Mary F. Lagod, his daughter. Mary's husband, Richard, was stationed at Fort Richardson at the time. The photo was taken at the Ft. Richardson museum. Richard first came to Alaska as a soldier serving at Fort Greely. Richard and Mary still live in Anchorage. *(Submitted by Lindalou Lagod)*

(LEFT) A WOMAN TO REMEMBER: Blanche McSmith, here with her daughter Kimberly, was a member of the first Alaska Legislature and the first black to serve in the Legislature. Born in Marshall, Texas., she had both a bachelor's and master's degree, the latter in social work from USC. Blanche came to Alaska in 1949 with her husband, William. They lived in Kodiak before moving to Anchorage. Over the years, Blanche McSmith was an energetic activist who gave thousands of hours to the civil rights movement and civic causes, often through service clubs. Her outstanding contribution was recognized in Alaska and nationally. "I think my husband came to Alaska to get me away from all my clubs," she laughingly told the Anchorage Times in 1958, "but I can't stay home. I tried to be a housewife, but it's just too dull." *(Submitted by the Blacks In Alaska History Project, George T. Harper, with permission)*

(LEFT) NIGHTMARE FOR ADULTS, DREAMLAND FOR KIDS: The Good Friday earthquake of 1964 dramatically rearranged the Turnagain section of Anchorage. These children found the lunar landscape the quake created irresistible. They made the area their play land. Anchorage Daily News cartoonist Peter Dunlap-Shohl remembers frequent sorties into the broken clay. His family lived nearby. Peter's father, Dr. Ted Shohl, took the photo facing east. He took many other photos of the effects of the quake, which did more than re-arrange the scenery. Two neighborhood children died. *(Submitted by Peter Dunlap-Shohl)*

(ABOVE) A PORKER'S PARADISE: Lloyd Schade of Homer is busy keeping a his hogs. The Schade family owned a slaughterhouse near Homer from 1964-1970. I the second licensed slaughterhouse in the state. On March 27, 1964 - the Good Frida earthquake - the family had more than 300 hogs on the farm. The quake prevented th delivery of the critters' food. Many of them had to be slaughtered earlier than expecte *(Submitted by Roxie and Lloyd Schade)*

(RIGHT) THE DESTRUCTION WAS EVERYWHERE: The damage from the 1964 Good Friday earthquake was frightening. For many people, everyday life was turned upside down. This home and the nearby car were doomed. The effects of the quake were felt as far away as Crescent City, Calif. The seismic wave following the quake drowned 10 people in the California community. Writer Stan Cohen says that 29 city blocks were damaged or destroyed. *(Submitted by Bruce Adams)*

(LEFT) HOME SWEET HOME: The Schade family looks so comfortable at home in this '60s photo. It wasn't always that way. Lloyd and Roxie came to Alaska in June 1958. They came on their honeymoon to homestead. As young newcomers, they lived in a tent while they built this home. From left to right, the family is Lloyd Schade, Douglas Schade (age 6), David Schade (8) and Faith Schade (18 months). Roxie is on the right. Today, Faith, her husband and children live in this very building. *(Submitted by Roxie and Lloyd Schade)*

EARTHQUAKE ALASKA!

33⅓ EXTENDED PLAY!!

COMPLETE
on the spot Earthquake sound

(LEFT) "OH MAN... OH... OH, BOY. I AM TELLING YOU....: It was Friday March 27, 1964, and Bob Pate, a salesman and announcer for KHAR, was in his living room reading. He was reading Mark Twain's "Letters From The Earth" when one of the biggest earthquakes in North American history hit Anchorage. Pate did the only rational thing a radioman could do: Turned on his tape recorder, an inexpensive model from J.C. Penney. And so began what Anchorage Times reporter David Postman called "a stream of consciousness narrative" that lasted almost 40 minutes. While the ground beneath his Blueberry Lane home rocked, Pate rolled tape. After the world returned to normal, Pate put the results on vinyl. This is the only known recording of the Good Friday quake. As Pate said, "Man everything is moving. You know that stuff in the cabinet.... And oh we scared the hell out of me man." *(Submitted by Selinda Grenn)*

(RIGHT) JOINING THE NEIGHBORS: It's Thanksgiving 1960 - or '61 - and these folks are gathered at the Schade homestead to enjoy the occasion. All are homesteaders. They are, left to right: Earl Hubbard, Johnny Burgess, Bob Gillis, Ann Gillis, Harry Schade, Darlene Sheldon and Bill Sheldon. *(Submitted by Roxie and Lloyd Schade)*

(RIGHT) OFF TO SEE A MINE: Sally Wienke crosses Peterson Creek near Juneau, April 19, 1970. She and Kristina Ahlnas were on their way to see an abandoned gold mine. Sally put her snowshoes to good use as the last stretch of the trail was covered with snow. Kristina, a native of Finland, lived in California and Washington before moving to Juneau. She later moved to Fairbanks. *(Submitted by Kristina Ahlnas)*

(LEFT) THE REFUELING STATION IS OPEN: Margaret Swanson, wife of the Chugiak postmaster Paul Swanson, is on the job at a "refueling" station for hikers. During the Kennedy administration, thousands of Americans, including many Alaskans, responded to the president's call for physical fitness by going on long hikes that were celebrated in the press. Swanee's Slopes was the unofficial name for the Swanson post office and the family's adjoining properties. Unfortunately, the child is unidentified. *(Submitted by Chugiak-Eagle River Historical Society)*

(LEFT) A PREMIER EVENT: Darrel Comstock and Cindy Pendleton share a moment to remember at the Westward Hotel in Anchorage, 1968. They were together for the premier of the Alaska outdoor film "Tayaru," which Darrel, Cindy and Cindy's husband, Bob, had all helped film and produce. "Tayaru" was conceived as a hunting film but became family fare after careful editing. The film's slogan was "You don't have to say it to see it." Darrel, an Anchorage television reporter, was in Cindy's judgment "the John Tracy of his day." In time, Darrel moved away. Cindy went on to teach in the Anchorage School District for 27 years. *(Submitted by Cindy Pendleton)*

(ABOVE) A DESTRUCTIVE SCENE: The Good Friday earthquake of 1964 wiped out these homes in the Turnagain section of Anchorage. It is amazing that only nine lives were lost in the city when the quake hit. Total damage to Alaska was estimated at more than $537 million with 60 percent of that figure in the Anchorage area. This photo was taken by the Alaska National Guard, which made a record of the damage. *(Submitted by Bruce Adams)*

(ABOVE) A COUPLE TO REMEMBER: Bill and Laura John lived in Northway, where this photo was taken in 1960. Dale and Bertha Wilson knew them well. Their daughter, Twila Wilson Palmatier, says the couple were warm, loving people who followed traditional ways. Good neighbors, good friends. *(Submitted by Twila Palmatier)*

(LEFT) A CLASSIC FAMILY POSE: The Hellenthal family gathers in their living room in the winter of 1961. From left to right: daughter Cathy (now Braund), son Marc, mother LaRue, father John and son Steve. John Hellenthal had a distinguished career in the law and public life. He was both a member of the Alaska Legislature (1959-63) and a member of the Alaska Constitutional Convention (1955). Cathy, Marc and LaRue all live in Anchorage. Steve lives in Billings, Montana. *(Submitted by LaRue Hellenthal)*

(RIGHT) ALL FOR NOME STAND UP AND HOLLER: The Nome High School cheerleading squad stands for the Nome Nugget photographer in the Nome high gym, 1967. They are, left to right, Clara Johnson, Jan Phelps, Jeanni Blanning (captain), Gail McIver Phillips (coach), Irene Oman, Mary Sackett and Bev Langton. Coach Phillips later went on to "coach" the Alaska Legislature - as speaker of the House of Representatives. *(Submitted by Gail Phillips)*

(RIGHT) A CLASSIC ALASKA SCENE: The blanket toss takes place this time in downtown Anchorage during the 1967 Fur Rendezvous. The Fur Rendezvous and the Fairbanks Winter Carnival were not complete without the blanket toss. The crowd especially loved it when some dignitary was sent flying toward the sky - and came crashing into the blanket. *(Submitted by Tam Agosti-Gisler)*

(LEFT) A RACER TO REMEMBER: Chuck Higgins stands next to his car at the Alaska Speedway, corner of DeBarr and Bragaw in Anchorage, 1962. The race ticket, dated 1964, was for a benefit for Alaska Crippled Children. In 1961, the Anchorage Times said Higgins and his rival Bert Shaw "dominated the ratings." Higgins commented "We are competitors - yes, enemies, no." The rivals were more or less neighbors, the Times said, because they both had businesses in the Muldoon-Boniface area. *(Submitted by Joy Higgins)*

(ABOVE) BIKERS ON PARADE: Dale Hillmer and fellow bikers built this float for the 1968 Fur Rendezvous parade. Dale and the boys promoted safe biking and gave the Alaska State Troopers their first two motorcycles for traffic control. The Last Frontier Motorcycle Club also patrolled the "Walk for Hope" and provided free groceries to needy families at Christmas and Thanksgiving. Dale currently lives in Wasilla. *(Submitted by Dale Hillmer)*

(ABOVE) AT THE SCIENCE FAIR: Barbara Walther stands near her science project, sometime in the '60s. The project involved a subject few adults know anything about - the antibiotic properties of lichens. Barbara is the daughter of Harold and Beryl Walther. Today, she lives in Wasilla. *(Submitted by Dale J. Walther)*

(ABOVE) STANDING WITH HIS CATCH: Oscar Vogel stands with his set net catch in 1961 near Point Possession. Vogel was not only a successful guide but he was an accomplished fisherman. Over the years, Oscar Vogel exemplified the Alaskan who could truly "live off the land." Even 40 years ago, many people who preferred life in the woods were forced to work for wages in "town" (any place that offered a paying job). Oscar's daughter, Mary Katherine Bell, lives in Soldotna. *(Submitted by Mary Katherine Bell)*

(LEFT) A COUPLE OF FURRY FELLAS: Duane Bernardy (left) and Bob Larsen (right) get the close inspection during the annual Fur Rendezvous beard-growing contest. The scene is downtown Anchorage, Fourth Avenue, looking west to east. The young woman is probably a Rendezvous queen contestant, perhaps her majesty. Both of the men worked at the Anchorage Westward Hotel, now the Hilton. *(Submitted by George Allen Bernardy)*

(RIGHT) AND THE WINNING BEARD BELONGS TO: Duane Bernardy won the Fur Rendezvous beard-growing contest in 1964, businessman's category. This was the last Rendezvous before the Good Friday earthquake that rearranged Anchorage. Duane was the bell captain at the Anchorage Westward Hotel, now the Hilton. His friend Bob Larsen, who also competed, was the hotel sales manager. Duane passed away in 1989. Bob lives in Anchorage. *(Submitted by George Allen Bernardy)*

(ABOVE) A PRINCE OF A HUNTER, A PRINCE OF A GUIDE: We've all seen pictures of Americans or Englishmen gone to India to hunt big game. Here's an Indian prince who came to Alaska to hunt. It's 1963, and he's modeling his success. The prince hunted near Stepan Lake northeast of Talkeetna with guide Oscar Vogel. Vogel was in the business from the '30s into the '60s. He was a real wilderness pro, admired as a guide and as a man. *(Submitted by Mary Katherine Bell)*

(LEFT) THE ROLL CALL OF THE STATES: Guide Oscar Vogel poses with various hunting trophies. The names of the states and countries illustrate the diversity of his clientele. Vogel was born in Bloomer, Wis. and came to Alaska in 1924, all of 19 years old. Vogel was a master of all the wilderness skills - hunting, fishing and trapping. He also wrote poetry under the pen name "Henry Rendal." His guiding headquarters was at Stepan (alternately Stephan) Lake east of Talkeetna. He married Bernadine Dickman of Piqua, Ohio, the daughter of one of his hunting clients. *(Submitted by Mary Katherine Bell)*

(RIGHT) COOKING UP A STORM: Gila (left) and Hannah Levine knead bread dough at their home in Hope. Clearly it's an activity the girls enjoyed. Their mother, Rosemarie, was not just their culinary arts teacher but their "school teacher" too. At the time, Hope did not have enough students for a school. The girls were educated via correspondence method. The family later moved to Seward. Rosemarie now lives in Anchorage. *(Submitted by Rosemarie Knecht)*

(BELOW) THE WALDRONS GATHER: Art Waldron Sr. founded Anchorage Sand and Gravel and had a going concern when this Christmas party photo was taken in 1961. All but two of the men, women and children in the photo are named Waldron. The Waldron family came to Alaska from Oregon in 1936. Art came to be superintendent of construction at the "new" city hall in Anchorage. The Waldron name is well known in Southcentral Alaska as the family contributed much to the making of modern Anchorage. Art Waldron Sr. is next to Santa Claus. Santa is Scotty Marshall-Pryde. *(Submitted by Art L. "Bill" Waldron)*

(ABOVE) SHOWING THE TOURISTS HOW IT'S DONE: Nels Swanberg Jr. demonstrates how to pan gold in the summer of 1966. Nels came from a mining family and spent many summers showing tourists the proper technique. Nothing makes a visitor happier than finding a little gold. Nels was born in Nome in 1902 and lived there until his death in 1991. His life paralleled most of the history of the town. Granddaughter Joy Berger lives in Anchorage. *(Submitted by Joy Berger)*

(ABOVE) A WHOLE LOTTA SHAKIN' GOIN' ON: Anchorage was a mess when the Good Friday earthquake hit in March 1964. This photo was taken from west to east along Fourth Avenue. Note the MacKay Building in the distance. Note the fresh rubble. It took quite a while to clean up downtown Anchorage - and to make it safe for those who worked there. *(Submitted by Robert DeLoach)*

(RIGHT) IF YOUR LEGS REACH THE FLOOR, DRIVE: An unknown cat gives his canine chauffeur instructions as they head home after a successful hunt. The two critters probably belonged to hunters who were with the Vern Gratias family, who hunted the Denali Highway for years. The family owns Gracious House, 52.8 miles east of Cantwell on the Denali. It's been a Gratias family business for 45 years, offering numerous services and recreational opportunities. Vern Gratias and his family moved to Anchorage in 1948-1949. *(Submitted by Sandra Kinney)*

(LEFT) THE REAL GUTTER BALL: The March 27, 1964 earthquake reduced a Kodiak bowling alley to rubble. All that was left at the scene was these balls and bags. On Kodiak Island and other nearby islands, 18 people died. The seismic wave that followed the quake destroyed more than 215 structures and left 600 people homeless. Many fishing vessels were destroyed and so were fish processing plants. Writer Stan Cohen says property damage in the area totaled more than $45 million. *(Submitted by Bruce Adams)*

(RIGHT) A BEAR HUNT AND THE KIDS HELPED OUT: The Ellis family stands in front of their plane. The occasion is a bear hunt near Katalla. Bill Ellis, Lorene Ellis and Lynn Ellis are in the back row. Cole Ellis and Kirk Ellis are in the front. The Ellis family had world-class wilderness experience as guides, hunters and bush pilots. They arrived in Anchorage in the summer of '54, moved to Nabesna in the spring of '62. Today, Lynn runs Ellis Air Taxi in Gulkana, Cole runs Nabesna Air and Kirk operates K-Air. The family also maintains a guiding business. *(Submitted by The Ellis Family)*

(LEFT) OPEN FOR BUSINESS AFTER THE QUAKE: The 1964 Good Friday earthquake did a lot of damage, especially to Alaska businesses. The Northern Commercial Co., for instance, was forced to leave its building and take up quarters in the old Buick Center on Anchorage's Fifth Avenue. In February 1965, the staff of the housewares/gifts department gathered together. They are Rica Swanson, Karl Hofner and Dean Alsobrook. Rica, now 98, lives in Anchorage. Karl moved away and Dean lives in Anchorage. Dean recalls that the N.C. store was located in the Buick Center for several years. *(Submitted by Josephine "Dean" Alsobrook)*

(RIGHT) HIS HOMEMADE CARIBOU: Thomas Finegan found some caribou hides and antlers near Lake Louise and converted the parts into a "real" caribou in 1961. Those days, hunters, especially from the military bases, had the reputation of "shooting up the country" and Finegan's boss worried somebody after caribou would blast the building in the background. Finegan recalls "I moved the caribou to the top of a nearby knoll. When we returned from a weekend in Anchorage, I checked to see how my caribou fared. Based on the condition of the pelt I would say that many shots had been fired at it that weekend." *(Submitted by Thomas Finegan)*

CENTENNIAL EXPOSITION FAIRBANKS, ALASKA

(LEFT) CELEBRATING THE PURCHASE: This postcard was printed in conjunction with the Alaska 1967 Centennial Exposition celebrating the 100th anniversary of the purchase of Alaska from the Russians. Here a variety of "old timers" in costume are, as the caption on the card explained, reliving "the fabulous, exciting days of Alaska's gold rush period." The "A-67" exposition drew many visitors and was enjoyed by locals and visitors alike. *(Submitted by Michael R. Barron)*

(ABOVE) THE REAL LION'S CLUB: Betty J. Combs and Merrill Chitty, owner of Chitty's Motel, pose with ("Princess") on the 1964 day she was introduced to the Mountain View Lion's Club. Texan Bill Hipp gave Princess to Betty and her husband, William Shirley, at an outdoor show in Chicago in 1959. The de-clawed Princess weighed 45 pounds. Betty and William left Alaska in 1964. Princess, grown to 200 pounds, stayed behind with Leon Brown of Brown Electric. Betty remembers Princess as tame and obliging, although on one occasion she destroyed an entire mattress in the manner that a house cat might shred a tissue. *(Submitted by Betty J. Combs)*

(ABOVE) A DEPARTED INSTITUTION: The Wrangell Institute played a role in educating Native youngsters for a number of years. It was a boarding school, similar to other boarding schools for Native youth, operated by the Bureau of Indian Affairs. This photo was taken in 1964. Alaska was going through many changes, political and social, that year as Alaska Natives began to move away from the boarding school model. The Wrangell Institute is no more. *(Submitted by Bruce Walker)*

(LEFT) GRADUATION DAY: The 1968 graduates of the Anchorage Community College practical nursing program gather for a group photo. Members of the class were Sarah Ball, Kathleen Barron, Edith Bergner, Joanne Clifford, Flora Davis, Charlene Gulbrandsen, Elizabeth Harris, Jeneanne Hulce, Ester Isman, Marie Starnes, Emogene Tofson and Roberta Webb. Eugene Short presented the Certificates of Completion. A tea and reception followed immediately. *(Submitted by Michael R. Barron)*

(RIGHT) JAZZIN' UP THE TRAIN: Fairbanks banker Bill Stroecker leads on the trumpet as a combo performs on the National Defense Transportation Association's annual celebratory outing on the Alaska Railroad. The trip - and the music - lasted from Fairbanks to Eielson Air Force Base and back. This trip was probably in the 1960s. Stroecker is a prominent Fairbanks banker who still plays a fine horn. *(Submitted by Ben and Kay Rosey)*

(RIGHT) YOUNG PEOPLE WHO CAME TO LEARN: Lt. Gov. H.A. "Red" Boucher is surrounded by student interns. They are in Boucher's office. It's the fall of 1971. Boucher remembers, "An intern was appointed to each department and they were to work with the commissioner to learn the mission of the department. It was Gov. Bill Egan's belief that young people should be more involved in state government. I had overall responsibility for coordinating the program." Boucher also remembers it was a joy to work with these young people. *(Submitted by H.A. Red Boucher)*

(LEFT) NOTTI ON A ROLL: Native leader Emil Notti was the Democratic candidate for congressman in a 1973 special election. Alaska's House seat became vacant after the death of Nick Begich. Notti put up a spirited campaign but lost to Don Young, who remains Alaska's congressman 30 years later. Young won the election by 1,821 votes. Note the phrase "Pipeline to Washington" on the side of the vehicle. As construction of the trans-Alaska pipeline approached, the word "pipeline" was everywhere. *(Submitted by Dr. Judith E. Samter)*

(LEFT) IT'S NOT DISCO, IT'S SQUARE DANCING: Some Homer folks got excited enough by the Homer Winter Carnival to try a little square dancing back in the 1970s. Snowshoes proved a challenge, but, hey, the only risk is that you might break your neck. The snow had to be hauled to the dance site downtown, Janie Myers remembers. She also recalls that one year the snowshoe dancers partnered on a sandy beach. Now that's serious square dancing. *(Submitted by Janie Myers)*

(RIGHT) A PIPELINE ROMANCE: Harry Crawford and his future wife, Gwen Perry-Crawford, get an inside look at the trans-Alaska pipeline. They were in Valdez, "probably in 1975" Harry recalls. Harry was an iron worker; Gwen was a laborer. He came to Alaska in 1975; she came in 1974. They married in 1982. Harry is a member of the Alaska House of Representatives from Anchorage. *(Submitted by Harry Crawford)*

(RIGHT) ORIGINS OF AN OUTDOOR ENTHUSIAST: Liz Geuss, Anchorage resident since 1962, hikes through the scenic Whittier wilderness with her 7 month-old son, Scott. The Geuss family, father Arthur, mother Liz and children Mark, Anne and Scott, also frequently went boating from Whittier on the weekends and enjoyed exploring the fjords. The entire family still has a great love of the outdoors and still lives in Anchorage. *(Submitted by Scott Geuss)*

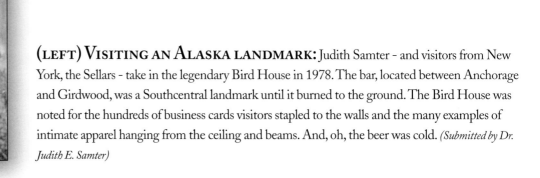

(LEFT) VISITING AN ALASKA LANDMARK: Judith Samter - and visitors from New York, the Sellars - take in the legendary Bird House in 1978. The bar, located between Anchorage and Girdwood, was a Southcentral landmark until it burned to the ground. The Bird House was noted for the hundreds of business cards visitors stapled to the walls and the many examples of intimate apparel hanging from the ceiling and beams. And, oh, the beer was cold. *(Submitted by Dr. Judith E. Samter)*

(RIGHT) A BASKET OF JOY: Melinda Palmatier slumbers in a birch bark baby basket in 1975. Jane Fix of Northway made the basket especially for her. Melinda's father, Dick, worked at the McLaughlin Youth Center. Mother Twila says the basket still hangs on the Palmatiers' wall. Melinda now lives in Anchorage. *(Submitted by Twila Palmatier)*

(ABOVE) NOW HERE'S A TRIO: Political leaders of yesteryear - and today - gather, sometime in the early '70s. Left to right Sen. Ted Stevens, Alaska Lt. Gov. H.A. "Red" Boucher, and Sen. Ted Kennedy. Boucher and Kennedy are Democrats, Stevens a Republican. Stevens and Kennedy are still in Washington and among the most influential senators. Red Boucher, who lives in Anchorage, has had a diverse career in politics, sports, the military, television and cyber communications. *(Submitted by H.A. Red Boucher)*

(LEFT) GETTING AN EARLY START: The Anchorage celebration of the nation's bicentennial got off to an early start in 1974 on the Delaney Park Strip. Left is Tam Agosti (Agosti-Gisler) who was Miss Teenage Anchorage, there for the program. Right is Ricky Boots. The bicentennial apparently was linked to the annual solstice celebration - something that probably happened in few Outside cities. (*Submitted by Tam Agosti-Gisler*)

(ABOVE) THE WHOLE DEPARTMENT WAS ON HAND: It's 1978 and the entire Fairbanks Fire Department is on hand for the retirement of Steve Childress (uniformed, center front). Presenting a plaque is City Manager Bob Wolting. Skip Causey, at the far left end of the last row, was one of the youngest firemen ever hired by the City of Fairbanks. He later went on to become battalion chief and was still working for the fire department when he passed away Dec. 15, 2000. (*Submitted by Donald Causey*)

(LEFT) TENTING TONIGHT AND TOMORROW NIGHT TOO: In the mid-'70s, Kristina Ahlnas found Fairbanks' rents inflated by dreams of an oil boom. So she purchased land and moved into a tent on June 15, 1975. She also took a class in log cabin construction and built a "practice cabin" while living in the tent. The "practice cabin" was really a cache. *(Submitted by Kristina Ahlnas)*

(RIGHT) AN EXAMPLE OF "PIPELINE IMPACT": Harriet Small stands in front of Ken's Pipeline Bar in downtown Fairbanks in 1977. The bar was one of many businesses that traded on the word "pipeline" during construction of the trans-Alaska pipeline. Harriet graduated from Oberlin College in June 1977 and hitch-hiked to Alaska, thinking she might stay a few years. She lived in Fairbanks for four years, and Juneau for eight years. For 12 years, she has lived in Anchorage. Harriet now is the secretary at Tudor Elementary School. *(Submitted by Harriet Small)*

(ABOVE) SUCCESSFUL IN SEWARD: The Gallagher family poses proudly with their catch in Seward, 1973. From left to right: George J. Gallagher, Scott Gallagher (age 10), Steven Gallagher (age 7) and Terry Gallagher (age 14). The Gallaghers took a yearly fishing trip to Seward, the self-styled "Fun Capital of Alaska." *(Submitted by Pat Gallagher)*

(LEFT) HAPPY ANNIVERSARY, AMERICA: Mary Primis (Pennino) waves a "grand old flag" on the bicentennial of the United States, July 4, 1976. The scene was downtown Anchorage, waiting for the holiday parade. The young lady's grandmother, Marion Gatzka, designed and sewed Mary's colonial dress and hat. The expression on Mary's face is delightful. *(Submitted by Diane Primis)*

(ABOVE) A COUPON STORY: You probably won't believe this. In the late '60s, the people of Homer needed a new fire engine. They didn't have the cash to buy one. But they discovered that if they sent Betty Crocker 5 million Crocker coupons, they would get a truck. That's not a misprint: 5 million coupons. For several years, the entire community saved coupons - and asked relatives Outside to save them too. Janie Myers says, "I wrote 150 Christmas cards a year asking for coupons." Eventually, the 5 million coupons were boxed and sent to Betty. Homer received this handsome truck in return. On this occasion, fire auxiliary members stand proudly in front of their "premium." It's probably no accident the truck is number 5. *(Submitted by Janie Myers)*

(RIGHT) ON TOP OF THE WORLD: Sixteen-year-old Tom Coghill, then a junior at Bartlett High School, stands atop Mt. McKinley June 26, 1976. Tom traversed the mountain up the West Buttress route and down the Muldrow Glacier. The young climber eventually graduated from the University of Alaska Fairbanks with a civil engineering degree. He now lives in North Pole, outside Fairbanks, and is an engineer with Alyeska Pipeline Service Co. on the trans-Alaska pipeline. *(Submitted by Bill Coghill)*

(ABOVE) CACHE? CABIN? IT'S STILL HOME: In October-November 1977 Kristina Ahlnas built this "practice cabin" on land near Fairbanks. She had taken a course on cabin building and wanted the practice. The "cabin" was a seven-foot by seven-foot cache. She lived in the cozy cache four years while building a true cabin. Kristina says she was warm at 40 below zero because she had a good sleeping bag and a good stove. Note: The ladder is 16 feet tall. *(Submitted by Kristina Ahlnas)*

'76 - TOP OF AMERICA

(RIGHT) MORE FISH THAN THEY EVER DREAMED: The Golden North Salmon Derby is underway, July 18, 1969. These boys are bringing in fish in Douglas at the end of the first day. Kristina Ahlnas, who took the photo, worked at the University of Alaska's marine station in Douglas at the time. *(Submitted by Kristina Ahlnas)*

(BELOW) FEELING THE SPIRIT: A happy crowd gathers on the Anchorage Park Strip for a "Jesus movement" rally in 1971. The movement stormed much of the United States and brought thousands of people to rallies like this one. At the time, some people saw these events as an alternative to hippie "Be-Ins" and rallies against the Vietnam War. Apparently these folks were enjoying themselves in sunny weather. *(Submitted by Barbara Dunaway)*

(LEFT) A TRAGEDY TO REMEMBER: In this dramatic photograph, Martin Strand captured the destruction of St. Michael's Cathedral in Sitka, Jan. 2, 1966. The cathedral was constructed in the Russian period by Bishop Innocent, pioneer Orthodox missionary. The fire did not destroy the Sitka Orthodox community, and a re-built St. Michael's was consecrated Nov. 21, 1976. *(Submitted by Grayce Oakley)*

(ABOVE) QUITE A CARIBOU: Lorene Ellis has her hands on a trophy caribou, 1976, in the Copper River country. Lorene and her husband, Bill, came to Alaska from Texas in 1954. They settled in Nabesna. Lorene was a true wilderness woman: She hunted, trapped and kept house to boot. For Lorene, the family says, there was no such thing as "going out to eat" or "calling for pizza." Self-reliance was the word. Lorene herself says "I wouldn't trade my life for any other life. I have enjoyed living here and I still enjoy it." *(Submitted by The Ellis Family)*

(RIGHT) QUITE A CAMP: Victory Bible Camp, 95 miles from Anchorage on the Glenn Highway, is halfway between Anchorage and Glennallen. The camp opened in 1947 after Sen. Bob Bartlett obtained 40 acres for the founders at $1.25 an acre. Today, the camp is more than 300 acres and can host a couple hundred campers at any one time. The camp is open year around. According to those familiar with the facility, Victory Bible Camp is the biggest nonmilitary camp in Alaska. Note Victory Peak in the background. *(Submitted by Vera Parkins)*

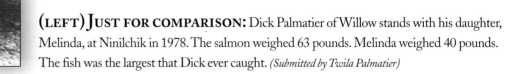

(LEFT) JUST FOR COMPARISON: Dick Palmatier of Willow stands with his daughter, Melinda, at Ninilchik in 1978. The salmon weighed 63 pounds. Melinda weighed 40 pounds. The fish was the largest that Dick ever caught. *(Submitted by Twila Palmatier)*

(LEFT) GETTING WATER IN WINTER: This is a classic Interior Alaska scene from Fox, north of Fairbanks. For years, Fairbanksans who want to improve their drinking water have come to the Fox spring to fill everything from 5-gallon jugs to coffee cans with cool, clear water, even in winter. People out for a drive in the country also will stop by, if only to satisfy their thirst with a coffee cup of Fox water. The date in this photo is Oct. 8, 1972. *(Submitted by Kristina Ahlnas)*

(ABOVE) LET'S HAVE A BIG HAND FOR THESE FOLKS: Anchorage Sand and Gravel had just put the new crusher in the background into operation. The company chose to memorialize the event in unusual fashion. Left to right, Robert Crook (engineer), Chuck Webber (local businessman, at one time president of the Chamber of Commerce), Art Waldron (founder of the company), Herb Lang (executive with the company), George Sullivan (mayor) and Wilda Hudson (local government representative). This was probably in the early '70s before unification of the city and borough, so Sullivan would have been city mayor and Hudson a member of the city council. *(Submitted by Mike Harned)*

(ABOVE) JUST SIGN RIGHT HERE: Two nuns put their "John Henry" on a beam that will become part of the foundation of Providence Hospital. It was a day to sign the cornerstone, and the nuns were there. Providence has played a major role in Anchorage and Alaska for many years. People come from all over the 49th state for medical care and appreciate the care and professionalism that greet them. *(Submitted by Providence Health System in Alaska)*

(ABOVE) GO KISS A MOOSE: Chuck Talsky is puckering up to kiss a moose as Steve Mahay of Mahay's Riverboat Service stands in the background. The men were on an Oct. 1978 fishing trip along the Talkeetna River, near the mouth of Clear Creek, when the young moose wondered down to the water. A wire service distributed copies of the photograph all over the country and Talsky received comments from people all over the country. Kiss a moose and folks will talk. *(Submitted by Steve Mahay and Chuck Talsky)*

(LEFT) NOW FOR A FEW WORDS: Jewel Jones addresses the Anchorage Black Caucus at their annual gathering in 1980. Sitting to her right is Sen. Mike Gravel who represented Alaska in Washington for two terms (1968-1980). A variety of civic and business leaders also are in attendance. Jewel Jones retired from the Municipality of Anchorage in 2003 after holding several social services leadership position. Her leadership was respected and appreciated throughout the community. *(Submitted by the Blacks In Alaska History Project, George T. Harper, with permission)*

(RIGHT) FLYING ON THE WATER: Helen Bohac gives a new dimension to water skiing as this floatplane pulls her along. The scene is Butterfly Lake, northwest of Big Lake, and the date is 1979. This kind of water skiing could be undertaken only on a lake that was isolated and uncrowded - which usually means available only by air. The airplane revolutionized transportation in Alaska. Here it's revolutionized sport. *(Submitted by Douglas Kent Bohac)*

Answering the call for twenty years.

ANCHORAGE DAILY NEWS HISTORY

The history of the Anchorage Daily News tells a story of perseverance and public service. The first publisher of the Daily News was Norman Brown. On January 13, 1946, volume 1, number 1 of the weekly Anchorage News rolled off the old Linotype hand-fed press from type set by hand. That first edition was 16 tabloid-sized pages, and while early editions were sold on the newsstands and distributed through the post office, there was no home delivery.

In 1948, the News went from being a weekly newspaper to being a daily, publishing 6 days a week. And in 1964 the Daily News converted from being an afternoon newspaper to being a morning paper. The change came only two weeks after the Good Friday Earthquake. The following year the Daily News began publishing Alaska's first Sunday newspaper.

Larry Fanning, a former San Francisco and Chicago newspaper editor, purchased controlling interest of the Anchorage Daily News and took over as publisher in June, 1967. When Fanning bought the Daily News, the circulation was 18,000. In 1971, 56-year old Fanning died of a heart attack in his Daily News office. Kay Fanning succeeded her husband as editor and publisher of the Daily News.

In 1976 the Daily News won the first of two Pulitzer Prizes for public service for a series of articles collectively called "Empire – The Alaska Teamster Story".

In 1979, McClatchy Newspapers of Sacramento, CA acquired 80 percent ownership of the Daily News. By late 1982, the weekday circulation of the Daily News passed 50,000 and the News became Alaska's largest newspaper. Circulation continued to grow, and by the summer of 1984, the News announced it would purchase land to build a new facility that would house all of its operations under one roof. In June, 1986, the Daily News moved into a new $30 million facility at 1001 Northway Drive.

The Daily News was again honored with the Pulitzer Prize in 1989 for a series called "People in Peril" which examined the problems of alcoholism and self-destruction affecting Native Alaskans.

The first online version of the Anchorage Daily News was launched at adn.com in 1996. In 2000 the entire newspaper was redesigned, offering a more consistent and usable format for readers. The paper's long history of community service was recognized when it was selected as the outstanding philanthropic organization in Alaska.

Despite downturns throughout the industry, the Daily News saw

circulation growth in 2001. A second website, Alaska.com, was launched that year. In addition, in 2001 the first volume of "Our Alaska" was published to showcase Alaska's history through photographs submitted by Daily News readers. "Our Alaska Volume II" was published in 2003, helping to preserve memories and document the many changes occurring in Alaska.

U.S. Army Signal Corps telephone line inspectors on the Richardson trail, which is now the Richardson Highway. (1926)

Construction crew (infantrymen) for the Washington-Alaska Military Cable and Telegraph System (WAMCATS) on Valdez-Fairbanks route. (1908)

WAMCATS hauling cable into Valdez. (1904)

Historic photos provided by U.S. Army

Connecting Our Great State

AT&T Alascom has been here since the beginning. When Captain Billy Mitchell initiated the first telecommunication system in Alaska back in 1900, so began the challenge of crossing 367 million acres and five varied regions to connect Alaskans to each other and to the rest of the world. More than 100 years later our company pride and commitment have inspired us to launch satellite systems, to link networks with over 5,000 miles of cable, and to construct more than 200 earth stations to serve even the smallest rural communities in Alaska.

Today AT&T Alascom employs about 300 people statewide who help connect and support over 200 million calls per year. We are also the company that delivers one of the largest satellite networks for telephone service in the world. AT&T Alascom is a way of life for most Alaskans— keeping us in touch with each other and the rest of the world.

AT&T Alascom

Contributor Index

CONTRIBUTOR INDEX

Anchorage Daily News

1001 NORTHWAY DRIVE, ANCHORAGE, AK 99508-2098

VOLUME II

Michael J. Sexton, President and Publisher

Robin Minard, Marketing Director

Michael Carey, Our Alaska Volume II Editor

Diane Karalunas, Designer

Ildiko Geuss, Community Relations Coordinator

Book Team Members: Kathy Bonney, Marc Bravo, Lonnie Burgener, Teri Cunningham, Jill Galbraith, Derk Inga,
Molly Killoran, Daniel Kremer, Dave Kuta, Lisa Mills, Don Ostrom, and Keven Stevenson

SPECIAL THANKS TO:

Leroi Heaven of Wasilla, Karen Erickson of Fairbanks, George Lounsbury of Fairbanks, John Bagoy of Anchorage,
Connie Gibbs, Marsha Miesch and everyone who submitted photos.
They really made a difference.

"Our Alaska Volume II: A Pictorial History of the Great Land and Its People" was a labor of love, and to all those who helped in any way, we express our appreciation. Special effort was made to ensure the accuracy of information accompanying these photographs. However, some information written on the backs of photographs and dates recalled by individuals may not have been exact. For historical accuracy, we welcome corrected and additional information. It will be forwarded to the appropriate individual, archives or museum. Please write to the Anchorage Daily News, Community Relations Department, P.O. Box 149001, Anchorage Alaska, 99514-9001. To order additional copies, please visit us online at adn.com or write to us at the address above.